PROJECT S.T.O.P.

SELF TAKING ON PREVENTION:

THE NATIONAL CRISIS
AND
CAUSE FOR CHANGE

LIFE CARE PLANNING

Christopher A. Lowery, DHSc, CLCP

Page Blank Intentionally

Project S.T.O.P.

Self-Taking On Prevention: The National Crisis And Cause For Change

All rights reserved. Printed in the United States of America. Available for purchase worldwide. No part of this publication may be reproduced, distributed, or transmitted in any form or by any means, including photocopying, recording, or other electronic or mechanical methods, without the prior written permission of the publisher, except in the case of brief quotations embodied in critical articles and reviews.

CAL Investments, Inc. books may be purchased for educational, business, or sales promotional use. For information, please write: Dr. Christopher A. Lowery, DHSc, CLCP, CAL Investments, Inc. d/b/a Healthways Services, P.O. Box 41217 Houston, Texas 77241

ISBN 979-8-9915688-4-5 (Paperback)
ISBN 979-8-9915688-6-9 (E-book)
ISBN 979-8-9915688-5-2 (Hardback)
ISBN 979-8-9915688-3-8 (Audiobook)

Library of Congress Control Number: 2024919572

FIRST EDITION 2024

Published by: CAL Investments, Inc. d/b/a Healthways Services
Dr. Christopher A. Lowery, DHSc, CLCP
PO Box 41217 Houston, Texas 77241
www.healthwaysservices.org

Manufactured in the United States of America. Distributed internationally.

Copyright © 2024 by Christopher A. Lowery, DHSc, CLCP

All rights reserved.

No portion of this book may be reproduced in any form without written permission from the publisher or author, except as permitted by U.S. copyright law.

Dedication

This book is dedicated to individuals who suffers from mental health, disabilities and disparities. In the silence of your struggles, may you find echoes of resilience. In the darkness of your doubts, may you discover sparks of hope and improve your quality of life. In the weight of your burdens, may you uncover wellsprings of strength. For every tear shed in solitude, know you are not alone. For every battle fought in silence, know your voice matters. For every step taken in shadows, know there is light waiting to guide you.

As you read this self-help book may your journey be met with understanding hearts, and may your path be paved with compassion and support for each other in unity.

With love and solidarity for everyone,

Christopher A. Lowery, DHSc, CLCP

Contents

Acknowledgments i

About the Author ii

Chapter 1: Breaking Barriers: An American Dream 3

    Present-Day America & Societal Challenges 3

    Overview of Diverse Cultural Narratives Explored in the
        Book 8

    Family Origin of Anger 10

Chapter 2: The Pandemic Accelerator 13

    The COVID-19 Pandemic 13

    Black American Communities 13

    Mental Health Impact & Responses Within Different
        Demographics 19

    First Responders & Coping Mechanisms 24

    Conclusion 25

Chapter 3: Social Media 28

    Who is the Prettiest of Them All? 29

    Video Games & Doomsday Scenarios 32

    Influencers Selling Hoaxes 33

Chapter 4: Unraveling Tensions – Immigrants 38

    American Immigrants 38

    Integration & Racism 43

    Women & Children: Vulnerabilities Amidst Migration 45

Chapter 5: Unraveling Tensions – Black Americans 48

    Disbelief & Heartbreak 49

    Stereotypes and Fears 51

    Ways to Improve Quality of Life Long-Term 58

Chapter 6: Unraveling Tensions – Jewish Americans 64

    Historical Trauma 64

    Healing & Recovery 67

    Stereotypes & Fears 68

    Ways to Improve Long-Term Quality of Life 76

Chapter 7: Unraveling Tensions – Muslim Americans 80

    Disbelief & Heartbreak 81

    Stereotypes & Fears 82

    Community Unity: Strategies for Overcoming Collective Challenges 90

    Pathways to Prosperity: Long-Term Solutions for Quality-of-Life Enhancement 92

Chapter 8: Unraveling Tensions – Latin American Perspectives 95

    Sorrow & Disbelief 95

    Stereotypes & Fears 96

    Pathways to Sustainable Long-Term Prosperity 102

Chapter 9: Threads of Resilience – Native Americans & Other Racial Groups 106

    Disbelief & Heartbreak 107

    Stereotypes & Fears 107

Pathways to Sustainable Long-Term Prosperity 114

Chapter 10: Unraveling Tensions – Asian Americans 117

    Impact of Perpetual Foreignness & Pandemic Stressors 117

    Historical Injustices: Displacement & Enduring Discrimination 119

    Anguish & Reassessment of Identity Amid Racial Divides & Incorporating Anger Management Research 121

    Coping Mechanisms & Strategies for Managing Anger 123

Chapter 11: Unraveling Tensions – Mexican Americans 127

    Dual Cultural Pressures Along the Borders of America 127

    The Struggle for Mexican American Identity 128

    Historical Injustices: Displacement & Enduring Discrimination 128

    Anguish & Reassessment of Identity Amid Racial Divides & Incorporating Anger Management Research 130

    Coping Mechanisms & Strategies for Managing Anger 133

Chapter 12: Decoding White Anger & Disparities – White Americans 136

    Understanding White Anger 136

    Historical Context 137

    Exploring Anger & Thuggish Behavior 140

    Health Disparities That Impact White Americans 146

Chapter 13: Building Bridges & Fostering Understanding 150

    Harnessing Empathy Across Cultures 150

    Intersections of Anger, Resilience, & Advocacy 151

    Journeys of Emotional Turmoil & Courage in Marginalized Communities 153

    The Imperative for Culturally Competent Mental Health
        Advocacy 155

    Promoting Understanding, Acceptance, & Unity 156

Chapter 14: Conclusion 160

References 162

Page Blank Intentionally

Acknowledgments

My heartfelt thanks and deepest gratitude to everyone higher power for guiding me throughout the entire process of writing this self-help book. Also, acknowledged are all the individuals facing mental health challenges, disabilities, and disparities. The resilience of all Americans going through many barriers inspires me to continue helping people understand how to overcome despair and frustration, aiding them in their quest to improve their quality of life. The work that I do every day as a board-certified life care planner encourages me to continue to advocate, counsel, educate, support and navigate resources for all Americans. I believe expanding access to mental health services is very important because it can truly make a difference between despondency and hope.

I encourage every reader to continue to fight for diversity, equity, and inclusion (DEI) for all, including in the realms of mental health, disabilities, and disparities. May your efforts serve as a catalyst for change and a source of empowerment.

Thank you all for your invaluable contributions and unwavering support.

About the Author

Dr. Christopher A. Lowery, DHSc, CLCP, is a renowned international board-certified life care planner practitioner and holds the position as a clinical health and rehabilitation consultant for Healthways Services dba of CAL Investments, Inc. He has over two decades of clinical experience and he delves into the intricacies of mental health initiatives for his telehealth clinical practice. In his self-help book entitled *Project S.T.O.P. - Self Taking On Prevention: The National Crisis And Cause For Change*. Dr. Lowery draws upon his extensive experience working with patients and clients battling various behavioral and psychological disorders. He offers profound insights and practical advice for his clinical practice to assist individuals in understanding and overcoming their inner struggles. With a compassionate and empathic approach, he explores topics ranging from anxiety, anger, depression, employment, occupational health, disparities, and biopsychosocial issues, such as illnesses, prevention, trauma, diseases, and more. By shedding light on the complexities of the human psyche, his groundbreaking work empowers readers to confront their demons and embark on a journey toward healing and self-discovery.

Dr. Lowery holds the following degrees: Bachelor of Science in rehabilitation studies from the University of North Texas (07), Master of Arts in human and health administration services from the University of Oklahoma (10), Post-Specialty Certificate in life care planning from Capital University Law School (12), Post-Master's Certificate in rehabilitation counseling from the University of Arkansas at Little Rock (14), and Doctor of Health Science in global health from Nova Southeastern University (16).

Dr. Lowery holds a board-certification in life care planning as a Certified Life Care Planner (CLCP) from the International Commission on Health Care Certification (ICHCC), which is accredited and recognized by the American National Standards Institute National Accreditation Board (ANAB). This prestigious certification attests to his qualifications and competence in health care delivery systems. ANAB's accreditation ensures that the certification process meets rigorous international standards, confirming his aptitude and expertise for his role as a practitioner.

Page Blank Intentionally

Chapter 1

Breaking Barriers: An American Dream

In striving for the American Dream, breaking barriers occurs from pursuing success and upward mobility when overcoming obstacles in the United States. The American Dream, a fundamental ethos embedded in the national psyche, promises the possibility of prosperity, social mobility, and a better life through hard work and determination. However, the pursuit of this dream has generated mental health issues from anger, anxiety, depression, and more, as individuals grapple with the pressure to succeed, the fear of failure, and the ever-present uncertainty of the future. These issues should not merely be an individual concern but also a societal undercurrent that reflects the broader challenges and expectations woven into the fabric of the American Dream.

The American Dream, initially rooted in the ideals of freedom and opportunity, has evolved, reflecting changing social, economic, and cultural values. The dream has been an aspirational force, driving individuals to overcome barriers. It becomes an impediment as societal expectations and economic realities shift. The tension between the pursuit of success and fear of failure has become a defining feature of the American experience. As people traverse the complexity of modern society, the idea of breaking barriers serves as a prism to study the subtleties and problems inherent in the continual pursuit of the American Dream.

Present-Day America & Societal Challenges

In the sprawling canvas of contemporary America, breaking barriers emerges as a pervasive force entwined with the complex challenges that define modern times. This chapter explores the layered network of societal fault lines, traversing the changing environment of modern America and the numerous issues that feed the pervasive sense of dread.

Additionally, mental health has become an overarching force or trigger in the vast fabric of modern America, carefully woven into the complicated difficulties that define people's days. These difficulties often cause daily stressors. Therefore, this exploration embarks on an insightful journey through multifaceted societal fault lines, illuminating the dynamics shaping people's collective psyches.

Racial justice has been the central focus of democratic enthusiasm and movement in recent years. The demise of 17-year-old Trayvon Martin on

February 26, 2012, had a profound impact on the politics and culture of America, reverberating through time despite its occurrence a decade ago. Following Martin's fatal shooting by George Zimmerman, a self-titled watcher in his Florida neighborhood, widespread protests were organized around the country as people called for accountability and justice.

The intensity of the protests escalated following Zimmerman's acquittal, and the hashtag BlackLivesMatter gained widespread popularity on social media. The aftermath ignited one of the most significant social movements in U.S. history. The democratic ethos is prominently evident in groups advocating for racial justice, emphasizing the ongoing struggle against systemic racism and injustice while showing the importance of holding individuals and institutions responsible. This energy demands justice in specific instances and signifies a growing cultural change.

The most evident example of this awakening occurred four years ago in the Black American community, with the killing of George Floyd in 2020 becoming a focal point. Therefore, as you continue to read this self-help book, you should find that the chapters will unpack the historical context of police brutality, disparities, and the disproportionate impact of the COVID-19 pandemic on most racial groups in the U.S. These matters have prompted me to spread notice and request a cause for change for everyone to take part because the U.S. is in a crisis. The protests and civil unrest following Floyd's death became emblematic of justified anger, demanding not only justice for Floyd's family but also a comprehensive overhaul of most continuing to relegate minorities to the position of second-class citizens, particularly Black Americans.

Minorities should no longer be considered second-class citizens. Equality is a fundamental human right, and I challenge all minorities to improve their lives daily by breaking barriers and promoting such changes. Laws were laid down in this country to protect all citizens, and everyone needs to start exercising them when events occur. Discrimination based on race, ethnicity, or any other factor is unjust and undermines the principles of fairness and inclusivity in society. It is the long-awaited time for everyone to improve their mental health, embrace diversity, and promote equal opportunities to benefit all, fostering more harmonious and prosperous communities.

In light of this need, I explore societal challenges faced by minorities. For example, in the U.S. healthcare system, pervasive medical racism disproportionately impacts Black Americans, evident in their undertreatment compared to their White counterparts—a disparity perpetuated throughout this country for years. This bias extends beyond clinics or hospitals, ignoring the impact of daily struggles like police brutality or racial profiling, substandard housing, polluted neighborhoods, and inadequate schools. Moreover, historical discrimination resurfaces, amplified during the pandemic, as Black Americans faced discrimination and abuse all across the U.S., particularly from healthcare professionals. I encourage more leaders in significant positions, such as attorney generals, hospital administrators, electoral officials, and other individuals involved, to start addressing discrimination in the medical field against Black Americans. I suggest the following systemic changes:

1. *Training and Education:* Implement antibias training for healthcare professionals to raise awareness and challenge unconscious biases.

2. *Diverse Representation:* Encourage diversity among healthcare providers to reflect their communities better.

3. *Policy Reforms:* Enforce strict policies against discrimination and hold healthcare providers and institutions accountable for discriminatory practices.

4. *Community Engagement:* Build trust and understanding between healthcare providers and Black communities through outreach programs and community involvement.

5. *Data Collection and Analysis:* Collect and analyze the data of healthcare disparities to identify areas of improvement and measure progress.

6. *Cultural Competency:* Promote cultural competency training to ensure healthcare providers understand Black patients' unique needs and experiences.

By implementing these measures, everyone can work toward a more equitable healthcare system that provides quality care to all individuals, regardless of race or ethnicity.

Additionally, it is essential to mention that everyone needs to start voting for electoral officials in offices that align with their values and priorities because it is crucial to implement necessary changes immediately. This need is apparent for the following reasons:

1. *Representation:* Elected officials have the power to represent the interests and concerns of their constituents. By voting for officials who prioritize addressing issues, such as discrimination in healthcare, society can ensure that these issues are brought to the forefront of policy discussions.

2. *Policy Making:* Elected officials can propose, pass, and implement

policies. By electing officials committed to reforming healthcare systems to reduce discrimination, society can push for legislative changes that promote equity, justice, and inclusion (EJI).

3. *Accountability:* Voters hold officials accountable for their actions and decisions through the electoral process. By voting for officials who prioritize addressing discrimination in healthcare, society can demand accountability and progress on these issues.

4. *Systemic Change:* Elected officials can enact systemic changes that can have a lasting impact on society. We can work toward building an inclusive society by voting for officials who advocate for structural reforms in healthcare and other sectors.

Ultimately, voting is a powerful tool for driving change and shaping the future of our communities and institutions. By participating in the electoral process, we can contribute to efforts addressing discrimination and promoting justice in healthcare and beyond.

Moreover, drawing inspiration from working in private practice and my experience as a board-certified life care planner, there is nothing more disturbing in this country today than an angry White American; in this book, I delve into racial tensions, economic inequalities, and political polarizations as shadows cast upon the American Dream. The exploration of the surge of mental health or health disparities within the White American community introducing the historical archetype of the angry White American, linking them to some of America's darkest moments.

High-profile prosecutions involving White American aggression, such as that of the Unite the Right event in Charlottesville, VA, in August 2017, illustrated how they deal with the racial conflicts that permeate modern culture. Chapter 12, intricately weaves these threads into a broader exploration of racial and White American anger.

Additionally, discussed within this book is how the COVID-19 pandemic has had a profound impact on White American communities, highlighting some of the health disparities within this population that most individuals are typically not aware of nor initiate discussions about; such disparities are not seen on news media, social media, or other platforms compared to certain other racial groups possibly resulting from perceptions of privilege, stigma, and shame as well as the fear of backlash, lack of awareness, or focus on other groups and not the self. These issues are concerning as they relate to the White population. After reading this book, the reader should be able to stop using *block mechanisms* (defenses, as discussed in more detail below) and address the White population's mental health crisis or disparities as opposed to focusing on other cultural groups. The White American population has problems, too; often, these problems are more significant than those of other racial groups. These issues are rarely discussed because of underreporting and data collection challenges, which contribute to why White Americans generally have better outcomes compared to other U.S. racial and ethnic groups. Other notable reasons entail a combination of historical, socioeconomic, and systemic factors.

As mentioned earlier, critical issues society faces are the use of block mechanisms. Block mechanisms are defenses to block accountability, often used as psychological mechanisms. White Americans often use these tactics to avoid taking responsibility for their actions by deflecting blame or expressing denial to others. They may use block mechanisms because of projection, rationalization, minimization, or avoidance. In order to explore this concept further, some standard defense definitions are listed below:

1. *Avoidance:* Avoiding or deflecting discussions about accountability by changing the subject, withdrawing from the conversation, or refusing to engage as a result of feedback or criticism;

2. *Blame-Shifting:* Redirecting blame onto others, either by exaggerating their faults or portraying oneself as a victim of circumstances;

3. *Denial:* Refusing to acknowledge one's role or responsibility in a situation, often by denying that the situation occurred or downplaying its significance;

4. *Minimization:* Downplaying the impact or consequences of one's actions, making excuses, or trivializing the harm caused;

5. *Projection:* Attributing one's thoughts, feelings, or behaviors to others, often to avoid facing uncomfortable truths about oneself;

6. *Rationalization:* Attributing or explaining one's actions to seem reasonable or acceptable, even if those actions may be harmful or unethical;

These defenses act as barriers that hinder personal growth, rational thinking, promotion of marginalized racial and ethnic cultural groups, acknowledgement of disparities, and lack development of successful relationships and societal progress within the White American population. These issues prevent the White population from taking ownership of their actions and addressing underlying issues. Please note that overcoming these defenses may require self-awareness, humility, participation in dismantling systemic racism, promotion of equitable access to opportunities, and a willingness to grow, mature, rationalize, and engage in honest reflection and dialogue about self.

Turning our attention to the Muslim American community, Chapter 7, explores mental health in response to the ongoing conflict, anger, and violence in Israel and Gaza, and the deep humanitarian crisis in the U.S. stemming from its ties to the Palestinian territories. The conflict between Israel and Palestine has significantly affected international and political relations but has also sparked a shift within Muslim communities (PH et al., 2023). Although the conflict has led to increased solidarity for Gaza, it has also raised societal awareness of political issues and spurred greater social involvement. These events have significantly contributed to the polarization of public opinions.

Opinions and behaviors tend to be shaped by the cultural and religious frameworks in people's lives. Globally, Muslim communities have fostered religious solidarity in favor of the resilience response of Gazans (PH et al., 2023). This solidarity among religious communities is stronger when rooted in religious rites, often manifesting in joint prayers and efforts to provide social assistance aimed at protecting and promoting peace for Palestinians. Efforts to provide donations and aid to the sufferers of the Israel–Palestine conflict is evident among Muslim communities all over the world.

Additionally, the book shifts to insights into Asian Americans and their mental health, unraveling the persistent perception of perpetual foreignness and the burden of conforming to the *model minority* stereotype. Consequences of misrepresentation by public figures and the feeling of being ignored despite significant contributions emerge as recurrent themes, underlining the roots of mental health problems among Asian Americans.

When acknowledging the validity of anger within these diverse groups, the narrative sets the stage for addressing challenges and seeking solutions. Emphasizing the need for leadership that encourages dialogue and unity highlights the potential role of influential voices within these communities in advocating for justice and systemic change. As the exploration concludes, it paves the way for a more in-depth understanding of anger's roots, its individual and collective dimensions, and strategies for effective management and transformation in the subsequent exploration.

Overview of Diverse Cultural Narratives Explored in the Book

Throughout the book, I aim to meticulously capture the mosaic of cultural narratives that intricately mold the American identity and attempt to dismantle or decrease mental health, discrimination, and disparities in the U.S. The rich array of immigrant experiences and the nuanced narratives of marginalized communities, each constituting essential threads in the complex emotions of the nation, are subjects of profound and scholarly examination.

Additional scholarly exploration lies in the narratives of marginalized communities. Through a lens focusing on historical injustices, systemic inequalities, and cultural determination, this examination goes through the intricate paths of communities frequently relegated to societal peripheries. The narratives considered herein provide a profound understanding of the emotional toll of prevailing societal structures, offering a poignant reflection on the collective mental health issues borne by those striving for recognition and justice.

The academic inquiry further delves into the dynamic narratives of Indigenous communities, whose stories are profoundly interwoven with the land itself. The inquiry acknowledges historical trauma, celebrates cultural richness, and addresses ongoing struggles, which constitute fundamental elements of this scholarly endeavor. I aim to shed light on the emotional complexities intrinsic to communities whose narratives form a foundational component of the American story.

The exploration extends into multifaceted narratives within racial and ethnic groups, ranging from Black Americans and African Americans to Asian Americans, White Americans, Latin Americans, and various religious groups. Another focal point of inquiry is the immigrant experience, a dynamic aspect within the American narrative. The thorough examination of diverse stories of those seeking refuge and opportunity on American soil aims to illuminate the profound influence of immigration on the collective emotional fabric. These narratives, characterized by strength and adaptation, offer nuanced insights into the intricate interplay between pursuing the American dream and the attendant mental health issues accompanying the journey. Meticulously, unraveling these threads serves to provide a profound understanding of the intricate interplay between cultural identity, societal expectations, and the pervasive undercurrents of mental health.

As we embark on this scholarly journey through diverse cultural narratives, the overarching objective is to deepen our academic understanding of how these stories exert influence and are influenced by mental health's undercurrents. The acknowledgment of the richness and complexity of these narratives may contribute to a more nuanced and empathetic comprehension of the multifaceted American identity within academic discourse and today's interconnected world. The challenges of mental health, discrimination, and societal disparities transcend boarders and cultures. As previously mentioned, this book aims to shed light on critical issues and offer actionable strategies to dismantle or decrease their impact, not only within America but globally.

The insights and approaches discussed here are designed to be adaptable, providing valuable lessons and tools that can be applied universally. The goal is to create a ripple effect that promotes mental well-being and restructuring equality, justice and inclusion (EJI) and/or diversity, equity and inclusion (DEI), encouraging a more inclusive and compassionate world for everyone.

Family Origin of Anger

You will notice that anger is another focal point throughout the book; therefore, the family origin of anger refers to how patterns of anger are shaped and transmitted within families across generations. Family dynamics, communication styles, cultural norms, and intergenerational experiences can influence these patterns. Some critical aspects of the family origin of anger include the following:

1. *Communication Patterns:* The quality of communication within a family can significantly impact how anger is expressed and resolved. Families encouraging open and respectful communication are more likely to address conflicts constructively, whereas families with poor communication skills may struggle to resolve anger-related issues.

2. *Cultural and Social Context:* Cultural norms and societal expectations regarding expressing emotions, including anger, can shape family dynamics. Some cultures may encourage the expression of anger to assert oneself or address grievances, while others may view anger as taboo or undesirable.

3. *Family Dynamics:* The structure and dynamics of the family unit can influence how anger is expressed and perceived. For example, families with authoritarian or controlling dynamics may suppress anger, leading to pent-up resentment and conflict, while families with more egalitarian dynamics may encourage open expressions of emotions.

4. *Intergenerational Transmission:* Patterns of anger can be passed down through generations as part of intergenerational trauma or learned behavior. Traumatic experiences, unresolved conflicts, and unaddressed issues from past generations can influence how anger is expressed and managed within the family.

5. *Modeling Behavior:* Children often learn how to express and manage anger by observing the behavior of their parents or community. If parents frequently display anger in aggressive or hostile ways, children may internalize these patterns and exhibit similar behaviors in their interactions.

Understanding the family origin of anger is critical in order to break cycles of dysfunction and promote healthier ways of expressing and managing anger within families or cultural groups. This understanding may come from recognizing and addressing underlying issues, developing effective communication skills, and seeking support from mental health professionals or other healthcare providers. By addressing these patterns at their root, families and cultural groups can create more supportive and harmonious relationships built on mutual respect and understanding.

Chapter 2

The Pandemic Accelerator

The COVID-19 Pandemic

The COVID-19 pandemic is often labeled the *Pandemic Accelerator*. COVID-19 has brought about significant disruptions to daily life, increasing stressors, uncertainty, and frustration for many Americans. Several factors may have contributed to the heightened anger during and after the pandemic. However, these issues are still ongoing, although COVID-19 no longer constitutes a global public health emergency.

More importantly, the COVID-19 pandemic not only laid bare systemic disparities within Black Americans and other minority communities but also emerged as a harrowing catalyst for a surge in mental health issues, such as anger, anxiety, and depression. The profound and multifaceted impact encompassed distressing health inequalities, staggering economic challenges, and formidable educational hurdles. This viral onslaught triggered an alarming spike in stress levels, pervasive mental health concerns, and a palpable sense of powerlessness within the communities mentioned above. The uncertainties surrounding health, economic stability, and resource availability have created a lot of worrying and disturbing situations that require immediate action to ease the escalating mental health crisis facing all racial groups and, more importantly, minority communities.

Black American Communities

Health Disparities

The unrelenting force of the pandemic laid bare a harsh and disturbing truth: the existing health disparities entrenched within the Black American community burgeoned into a deeply alarming crisis, reaching critical proportions. The heightened prevalence of preexisting health conditions, spanning diabetes, hypertension, and respiratory illnesses, cast a pervasive shadow over this demographic, rendering them exceptionally vulnerable to the severe consequences of COVID-19. This grim reality was further compounded by a distressing lack of access to quality healthcare and entrenched systemic disparities that intensified these formidable challenges.

In the face of the viral onslaught, Black Americans found themselves disproportionately targeted, experiencing significantly higher rates of hospitalization and mortality in stark comparison to other racial and ethnic groups. The statistics painted a chilling portrait of healthcare inequities, illuminating the urgent need for immediate and comprehensive interventions to rectify the deeply embedded imbalances plaguing the healthcare system for Black Americans.

The distressing lack of accessible healthcare resources left many within the community grappling with a stark choice between delayed or insufficient medical care, exacerbating the severity of cases and contributing to an elevated mortality rate. Systemic disparities in socioeconomic factors, education, and healthcare infrastructure underscored the pervasive nature of the challenges faced by Black Americans.

The crisis highlighted the imperative for an immediate overhaul of healthcare policies, targeted investments in community health infrastructure, and a concerted effort to address the systemic inequities exacerbating the impact of the pandemic. This multifaceted approach aimed to mitigate the immediate health crisis and foster long-term courage within the Black American community against future health challenges. In its stark revelation of systemic vulnerabilities, the pandemic catalyzed a call for sweeping reforms and a reevaluation of public health strategies to ensure a more equitable and resilient future for all communities.

Economic Inequities

The pandemic placed many within the Black American community in the crucible of essential jobs, requiring physical presence in sectors like healthcare, service industries, public transportation and small business owners. However, as the relentless wave of lockdowns swept in, the specter of job losses loomed ominously, and economic instability cast a long, foreboding shadow. The financial strain on Black Americans deepened to a profoundly alarming degree, exacerbating already severe economic disparities that had long persisted. The inability to transition to remote work and the higher likelihood of employment in positions with minimal job security have added to the weight of these challenges.

The accompanying economic instability carved out a terrain of misery, anger, depression, anxiety, and other health conditions for Black Americans and families, who faced the daunting job of tackling a maze of financial challenges. The palpable strain on households underscored the pressing need for targeted interventions and equitable economic policies to address the disparities perpetuated by the pandemic. The challenges revealed by this economic upheaval demanded a collective response, prompting a reassessment of labor practices, social safety nets, and economic support structures to build a more resilient foundation for Black American communities. The economic fallout reflected preexisting disparities and a rallying call for transformative change to ensure a more equitable and secure future for all.

Small Businesses. Black-owned small businesses were significantly affected by COVID-19 pandemic, particularly restaurants, retail shops, hospitality, and other service-based enterprises. The substantial challenges during the COVID-19 pandemic, included severe declines in revenue due to lockdowns, reduced consumer spending, and operational restrictions. Other challenges consist of access to financial support, higher closure rates, disparities in recovery, and community impact. Therefore, more efforts need to be implemented towards initiatives and advocacy for equitable access towards resources and opportunities regarding Black owned businesses across U.S. to target a more inclusiveness (DEI).

Education Challenges

According to Golden et al. (2023), many Black American students' educational aspects during the pandemic were marked by a stark and unsettling reality, such as a lack of access to necessary computer technology, high-speed internet, and an environment conducive to learning. Even though social class and race in the U.S. are no longer mutually exclusive, the history of political and economic oppression of Black Americans continues to pervade aspects such as education. The wealth gap between Black and White people in the U.S. continues to remain steady, the former of which was one of the communities impacted most severely by the COVID-19 outbreak, further worsening the digital divide.

Although access to technology was nowhere near the same as before the pandemic, the outbreak has disproportionately and negatively impacted vulnerable social groups. Computer ownership in American households during the pandemic was at least 92%; however, the ownership rates were the lowest among Black households (Golden et al., 2023). Even though many had access to at least one computer, it did not automatically equate to active Internet subscriptions or quality access to these connections. For many of these household areas, limited access to the Internet severely impacted the quality of learning they could attain.

This pervasive sense of inequality underscored the urgent need for systemic educational changes to dismantle barriers and ensure equal opportunities for all students. The disparities in access to educational resources created a distressing environment, contributing to an overarching sense of emotional distress among Black American students. The frustration stemming from this educational divide went beyond the immediate challenges of virtual learning, serving as a poignant reminder of systemic inequalities deeply rooted in the education system.

As minorities dealt with the academic challenges and emotional tolls of maneuvering an unfair educational perspective, the need for radical reforms in education policy, infrastructure, and support systems grew more pressing than ever. The pandemic laid bare the fault lines in the system, compelling a collective reevaluation of educational practices. Therefore, leaders should build a future for every student, irrespective of their background, ensuring they have equitable access to the tools and resources necessary for academic success.

Mental Health & Health Impact

Beyond the relentless assault on physical health, the pandemic unfurled a devastating impact on the mental well-being of Black Americans. The ceaseless stress stemming from health concerns, economic instability, and the profound loss of loved ones delivered an intensely disproportionate blow to the community. The limited access to health resources created a distressing situation of amplifying anger, anxiety, depression, and various mental health and physical health challenges. The cumulative weight of these stressors underscored an urgent and dire need for highly tailored healthcare support and resources specifically designed to alleviate the intensified emotional toll experienced by the Black American community.

The many health repercussions became an intricate web of interrelated difficulties, reflecting the pandemic's multidimensional influence on the population. The emotional distress was not only a reaction to immediate circumstances but also a manifestation of deep-seated societal and systemic issues that have long affected the well-being of Black Americans. The urgency for targeted health interventions became a rallying cry for comprehensive and culturally sensitive approaches to address the unique challenges faced by the community during and in the aftermath of the pandemic. The call for health support extended beyond a temporary response, emphasizing the need for sustained and long-term strategies to build spiritedness within the Black American population.

Since COVID-19, the prevalence of anxiety and depression worldwide has increased as high as 30%, a rise from 25% in February 2020 (Mahmud et al., 2023). The pandemic has also been linked to the greater prevalence of psychological distress and mental illness, resulting in more significant confusion, stress, insomnia, and anger within the population. Stress and fears have also been heightened anxiety and fears of premature death, especially among individuals suffering from health comorbidities, weak immune systems, and chronic underlying conditions.

Community Impact

The pandemic's unending misery severely stressed traditional support structures, often thought to provide a lifeline during difficult times. The Black American community faced significant challenges during COVID-19 pandemic, particularly impacted, as funerals, gatherings, community events—critical sources of connection—have been disrupted, leading to a pervasive sense of sadness over this population social and emotional well-being. The isolation and profound loss experienced during the pandemic underscored the importance and irreplaceable nature of community support structures.

This sad reality emphasized an acute need for targeted interventions to address the community's specific and heart-wrenching challenges. The depth of sorrow woven into their experiences demanded a nuanced approach, recognizing the intricate layers of grief; and the unique cultural and communal ways of support was traditionally sought and received. The appeal for intervention went beyond acknowledging loss; it became a cry for a compassionate response, acknowledging the complex fabric of emotions and cultural subtleties buried in the mourning process.

As the pandemic disrupted the customary avenues for solace and communal healing, the pressing need for innovative and culturally sensitive support approaches emerged. It became evident that traditional support systems, strained as they were, required reinforcement and adaptation to address the evolving needs of the Black American community. The grief experienced during the pandemic was not merely an individual burden but also a collective sorrow that necessitated a communal, compassionate, and culturally attuned response to begin the healing process. As Isasi et al. (2021) explained, access to education, food, housing, and transportation determines the population's health. More research must be conducted to understand how the social needs of vulnerable members of society are captured and how the right resources are identified and made available to those who need them. U.S. public health resources continue to be underfunded, leading to a lack of coordination in effective services supporting the mental and physical well-being of communities.

Vaccine Hesitancy

Historical vaccine hesitancy among Black Americans is deeply rooted in the profound wounds of past injustices, prominently embodied by the infamous Tuskegee Syphilis Study and other instances of medical exploitation. These haunting historical traumas have cast a long and enduring shadow on the community's trust in healthcare institutions, erecting skepticism as a formidable barrier against embracing vaccination efforts. Addressing this deep-seated distrust and ensuring equitable vaccine distribution became paramount in the battle against the pandemic.

Intensive and comprehensive efforts were undertaken to rebuild trust, disseminate accurate information, and actively involve community leaders in vaccination campaigns. Leaders played a pivotal role in bridging the gap and addressing the lingering vaccine hesitancy within the Black American population. Their presence and advocacy provided a crucial bridge between communities and healthcare institutions, fostering an environment of transparency and understanding.

The historical scars add a poignant layer to the contemporary struggle for trust and equitable healthcare access during these challenging times. Initiatives sought not only to encourage vaccination but also to acknowledge and rectify the systemic issues that fueled skepticism, recognizing the validity of the concerns rooted in the historical context. The collaborative efforts were aimed at administering vaccines as well as healing the wounds of the past, emphasizing a commitment to an equitable and just healthcare system that continues to respect the dignity and agency of every individual, particularly within the Black American community (Pourrazavi et al., 2023).

Activism & Resilience

Grassroots movements and community organizations emerged as beacons of hope during the pandemic, playing an indispensable role in addressing immediate needs, ranging from essential food distribution to promoting vital health education. The tenacity throughout these challenging times demonstrated the Black American community's strength and unrelenting dedication to face problems together. Rather than surrendering to hardship, communities sparked more participation and strong advocacy in the face of the pandemic.

This grassroots momentum aimed to address immediate concerns and advocate for profound, long-term, and systemic changes targeting the root causes of pervasive disparities. The efforts signaled a powerful drive toward lasting societal transformation, with communities shaping a more equitable and just future. While revealing deep-seated disparities, the pandemic became a turning point where grassroots initiatives transformed into powerful agents of change, challenging systemic inequities and paving the way for a more inclusive and resilient society.

The collective strength displayed by these grassroots movements emphasized the capacity of communities to lead their transformation. Their strength underscored the importance of community-driven solutions, and the immense and positive impact local initiatives can bring. Although challenging, the pandemic became a testament to the strength that emerges when communities unite to address immediate needs and advocate for broader, lasting systemic changes.

Mental Health Impact & Responses Within Different Demographics

The toll of COVID-19 on mental health was harrowing, having deeply penetrated diverse demographics with varying degrees of intensity. As the pandemic unfurled, the relentless onslaught of pervasive uncertainty, health concerns, economic instability, and isolation ushered in a surge of mental health challenges. Anger, depression, and anxiety, in particular, elicited overpowering emotional reactions, creating an unpleasant and complex terrain. Individuals from marginalized communities bore the brunt of compounded stressors, with existing disparities mercilessly magnified by the pandemic's unforgiving force. The economic fallout, limited access to healthcare, and educational disruptions disproportionately afflicted vulnerable populations. These issues heightened their experiences of anger and anxiety to a truly alarming degree.

Responses to this mental health crisis were diverse yet underscored by an intense urgency. Communities mobilized fervently to address the unique needs of their members, as grassroots movements, community organizations, and mental health advocates played pivotal roles in providing desperately needed support and resources. Culturally sensitive interventions and targeted mental health programs became not just beneficial; but essential components of the response, acknowledging the diverse and profound ways in which communities grappled with the escalating mental health challenges. Addressing the aftermath of the pandemic highlighted the importance of a comprehensive and inclusive strategy for tackling its long-term and persistent effects on mental health, notably the elevated and problematic levels of anger, depression, anxiety, and other conditions across diverse populations.

The Impact of the COVID-19 Pandemic on other American Communities

Latino/Hispanic Communities

U.S. Latino and Hispanic communities have faced distinctive and interconnected challenges during the COVID-19 pandemic. Their overrepresentation in essential yet vulnerable sectors heightened the struggle, making them vulnerable to increased risks of exposure. Language barriers compounded the difficulties, as significant obstacles impeded access to critical information and essential services. Limited healthcare access exacerbated existing disparities, leaving many without timely medical assistance, while economic instability added another layer of complexity. Job losses and income disparities disproportionately affected these communities, intensifying financial strain and worsening the overall impact.

This web of challenges created a complex and daunting scenery, underscoring the urgent need for targeted support. Recognizing the unique burdens faced by the Latino and Hispanic populations became paramount, necessitating comprehensive interventions that address the intricate intersection of linguistic, economic, and health disparities. The pandemic exposed vulnerabilities and emphasized the imperative for equitable and culturally sensitive measures to alleviate the overwhelming challenges faced by these communities during trying times.

Asian American Communities

During the COVID-19 pandemic, Asian American communities experienced health and economic hardships, along with a worrisome spike in xenophobia and bigotry. This population was profoundly affected by lockdowns—such as hospitality and service industries—intensified economic hardships, creating an additional layer of vulnerability. The surge in anti-Asian sentiment imposed an emotional toll, further complicating the already complex navigation of the pandemic.

This convergence of health, economic, and societal challenges underscored the imperative for comprehensive support mechanisms. U.S. Asian American communities have found themselves grappling with multifaceted impacts that demanded a holistic response. The need for support extended beyond traditional economic relief, emphasizing the importance of addressing the emotional toll of discrimination and xenophobia. The pandemic laid bare the interconnectedness of various challenges faced by Asian American communities, highlighting the urgent need for inclusive and culturally sensitive support systems to facilitate recovery.

Native American/Indigenous Communities

U.S. Indigenous communities have confronted distinctive and formidable challenges during the COVID-19 pandemic. A unique set of barriers comprised limited healthcare access, a higher prevalence of preexisting health conditions, and disruptions to cultural practices. Overcrowded reservation living conditions further exacerbated these challenges, creating conditions conducive to the virus's rapid spread within tight-knit communities.

This confluence of factors underscored the urgent necessity for targeted interventions and cultural sensitivity. Indigenous communities found themselves at the intersection of health disparities, cultural preservation, and environmental factors, demanding a nuanced approach to address their specific and pressing needs. The pandemic's far-reaching impacts revealed the systemic vulnerabilities faced by Indigenous populations and emphasized the imperative for comprehensive strategies that respect and integrate cultural practices. The call for intervention has extended beyond immediate healthcare concerns, highlighting the importance of preserving and protecting the cultural fabric of these communities as an integral part of the pandemic response.

Low-Income Communities

Low-income communities, irrespective of racial or ethnic backgrounds, grappled with significant and interconnected challenges during the pandemic. This impact was compounded by limited access to healthcare, placing an additional burden on those already facing economic hardships. High-risk employment heightened the vulnerability of individuals within these communities, exposing them to increased health risks. The difficulties of adapting to remote learning further exacerbated educational disparities, creating a multifaceted and complex situation for those with limited economic means.

This web of challenges underscored the urgent need for comprehensive support mechanisms. It became evident that addressing the impacts of the pandemic on low-income communities required a holistic approach, considering the intricate interplay of economic, health, and educational factors. The call for intervention has extended beyond immediate relief, emphasizing the importance of implementing sustainable solutions that empower individuals within their communities that face potential challenges. The pandemic laid bare the systemic inequities low-income communities face, thereby demanding thoughtful and inclusive strategies to ensure their well-being and access to essential resources.

White American Communities

The COVID-19 pandemic has impacted White American communities in various ways. They experienced the direct health effects of COVID-19, with many falling ill, requiring hospitalization, and, tragically, losing their lives to the virus. As mentioned above in this book, while racial and ethnic minority groups were disproportionately affected by COVID-19 in terms of infection rates and mortality, White Americans have not been immune to the physical toll the pandemic exerted. Some issues that White Americans experienced include limited access to the economy, mental health issues such as stress and anxiety, and difficulties with healthcare, education, and social dynamics.

Economic Impact

Job Loss & Financial Strain. Many White Americans faced layoffs or reduced working hours due to lockdowns and economic slowdowns caused by the COVID-19 pandemic. This issue led to significant strain for numerous households, with individuals struggling to meet financial obligations, such as bills, mortgages, or rent payments. The sudden and unexpected nature of these economic challenges exacerbated stress and uncertainty for many families, highlighting the vulnerability of even middle-class households to unforeseen disruptions.

Small Businesses. White Americans owned many small businesses, including restaurants, retail shops, and other service-based enterprises. They faced substantial challenges during the COVID-19 pandemic, experiencing significant losses in revenue, with some being forced to shut down their businesses permanently. The pandemic-related restrictions reduced consumer spending, while supply chain disruptions created a challenging environment for small business owners, impacting their livelihoods and the broader communities that relied on these businesses for goods and services.

Mental Health

Isolation & Loneliness. The social distancing measures and lockdowns implemented during the COVID-19 pandemic resulted in heightened feelings of isolation and loneliness for many White Americans. This issue was especially pronounced among older adults and individuals living alone. The inability to socialize with friends and family, participate in community activities, or even engage in simple daily interactions exacerbated feelings of loneliness. As a result, mental health concerns about depression and anxiety, among other various challenges, became more prevalent within this population, underscoring the broader toll the pandemic had on mental health.

Anger, Depression, & Anxiety. The pervasive uncertainty brought about by the pandemic, coupled with health fears and financial insecurities, led to heightened levels of anger, depression, stress, and anxiety among many White Americans. The constant news updates about the virus, coupled with concerns about job security and the health of loved ones, created a persistent sense of unease. This chronic stress had a tangible impact on mental well-being, leading to sleep disturbances and concentration difficulties, even exacerbating preexisting mental health conditions for some individuals.

Medical Healthcare

Access to Healthcare. Despite White Americans' better access to healthcare compared to other racial and ethnic groups, this access is often hard to track due to underreporting and inconsistencies. White Americans may be less likely to report certain health conditions or seek healthcare services due to stigma, denial, minimization, and blame-shifting. This underreporting can lead to gaps in data collection and inconsistencies in healthcare surveillance.

Vaccination. At the onset of the vaccine rollout, there was noticeable hesitancy among specific segments of White Americans, influenced in part by regional differences and political affiliations. As the vaccination campaign progressed, rates improved across the board. However, disparities in vaccine distribution and access continued to be a concern, with some areas and populations having more access to vaccines than others. These disparities contributed to uneven vaccination rates and posed challenges in achieving widespread immunity.

Health Disparities Within the Population. Despite their overall better health outcomes compared to some other racial and ethnic groups, White Americans still experienced disparities in healthcare access, quality, and outcomes. Specific subgroups within the White population, such as rural residents, low-income individuals, and older adults, faced barriers to healthcare that contributed to disparities during the pandemic that they are still burdened by to this day.

Education

School Closures. Many White American students faced educational disruptions with the shift to remote learning. Parents found themselves navigating the complexities of working from home while assisting their children with online learning, creating additional stress and other challenges. The digital divide also became more pronounced, as not all families had equal access to the necessary technology or internet connectivity for effective remote education.

Higher Education. College students, predominantly White Americans, experienced significant disruptions due to the pandemic. Universities shifted to online instruction, altering the traditional college experience. Many students missed on-campus activities, internships, and social interactions essential for personal and professional growth. Additionally, the uncertainty surrounding graduation and future academic plans added to these students' stress and challenges during this period.

Social Impact

Community Engagement. The pandemic caused a notable decline in community events and gatherings, influencing White Americans' social engagement and connection opportunities. Many traditional community activities, such as festivals, fairs, and local meetings, were canceled or moved online. This shift disrupted the sense of community and social bonding that many White Americans value, further exacerbating feelings of isolation and detachment during these challenging times.

Volunteerism & Charitable Giving. Despite the hardships brought on by the pandemic, many White Americans supported their communities through volunteer work and charitable donations. Recognizing the struggles of their neighbors and local organizations, individuals contributed their time, skills, and resources to help where it was most needed. This collective effort showcased the resilience and compassion of many White Americans, highlighting the importance of community solidarity during times of crisis.

First Responders & Coping Mechanisms

The initial days of the pandemic unfurled an atmosphere of pervasive uncertainty, heightened health concerns, and unprecedented work demands. In the realm of first responders, the toll of the COVID-19 pandemic has been particularly profound, unveiling a unique set of challenges that demanded resilient coping mechanisms. For these dedicated individuals, grappling with the surge in mental health challenges, including heightened anger and anxiety, became an intrinsic part of their daily reality.

The relentless exposure to traumatic situations intensified the impact on mental health within this demographic, the constant fear of infection, and the strains on personal well-being. The emotional toll extended beyond the workplace, permeating personal lives and straining relationships. The economic uncertainties and fear of contagion added a layer of complexity to an already demanding profession.

Amidst these challenges, first responders exhibited remarkable courage, implementing coping mechanisms to truly gain an understanding of the pandemic and the significant increase in mental health crises. Peer support networks played a pivotal role, providing a crucial outlet for shared experiences and emotional expression. Mental health awareness initiatives, tailored to the unique needs of first responders, emerged as essential components of the coping strategy. Additionally, access to specialized mental health resources and counseling services became paramount, acknowledging the profound impact of the pandemic on the well-being of those who serve on the front lines.

As we reflect on the experiences of first responders during the pandemic, it becomes evident that addressing their mental health challenges necessitates a comprehensive and proactive approach. First responders exemplify the utilization of coping mechanisms across all populations mentioned in this book; therefore, tailored interventions are highlighted to support their mental health and well-being amidst unprecedented challenges.

The Causality of Empathy

Empathy, a visceral force that transcends individual boundaries, emerged as a linchpin in the collective reaction to the crisis, sparking a cascade of interconnected impacts on individuals, communities, and societies. As the virus proliferated, empathy became a driving and transformative influence. Its causality unfolded dynamically, shaping how individuals grappled with profound challenges, communities rallied with unyielding solidarity, and societies redefined norms in the wake of upheaval. In the crucible of the pandemic, empathy was not just a passive emotion but also a catalyst that propelled action through understanding, pervasive uncertainty, staggering loss, and systemic shifts.

In the wake of this unprecedented crisis, understanding the roots of empathy becomes a deeply felt expedition, plunging us into the profound and complex fabric of collective humanity. It is a fabric woven with strands of empathy, serving as a soothing remedy and fiery catalyst while propelling us through the forge of these demanding times.

Resentment & Distrust Toward Institutions

In the wake of the COVID-19 pandemic, the palpable emergence of resentment and distrust toward institutions casts a pervasive shadow over society. As the crisis unfolded, institutions once revered as pillars of stability faced unprecedented challenges. These challenges birthed a complex interplay of emotions and attitudes from the public.

The erosion of trust in governmental bodies, healthcare systems, and public health agencies became a palpable undercurrent, exacerbated by misinformation, conflicting messages, and perceived lapses in crisis management. The repercussions of these sentiments rippled through communities, shaping individuals' behaviors and influencing broader societal perceptions.

Conclusion

The chapter undertook an intense examination, unraveling the intricate factors that fueled people's sentiments and exploring the causes and consequences of their resentment and distrust. From the perceived mishandling of information to issues of transparency and accountability, it scrutinized the multifaceted nature of these emotions and their lasting impacts on public perception. Understanding the aftermath of the pandemic, requires a comprehensive knowledge of the complex interplay between individuals and organizations tasked with protecting global health. Through poignant narratives, critical analysis, and the exploration of alternative paradigms, this chapter aimed to illuminate the intensity of resentment and distrust toward institutions that emerged after the global crisis.

The symphony of the COVID-19 pandemic, etched with the ink of tough times, reveals a compelling narrative for all communities, marked by health crises, economic tribulations, and educational challenges. Nevertheless, within the haunting notes of anger and anxiety, there lies an opportunity for a harmonic resolution. The conclusion beckons a cadence of change, calling for harmonizing healthcare policies, economic structures, and educational systems. The chapter underscored the imperative of creating culturally sensitive mental health interventions and reinforcing traditional community support systems. Addressing historical vaccine hesitancy requires vaccination efforts and a commitment to healing past wounds. The call demands grassroots movements and community spirit to compose a transformative opus, steering us toward a future of equity and understanding.

Chapter 3
Social Media

In today's interconnected world, social media has fundamentally transformed how we interact with others and perceive ourselves. What once began as platforms for connecting with friends and sharing updates has evolved into a digital ecosystem that profoundly shapes our thoughts, behaviors, and emotions. Although social media offers numerous benefits, such as instant communication, access to information, and opportunities for self-expression, it also presents a host of mental health challenges that cannot be overlooked.

At the heart of the issue lies the relentless exposure to curated content, carefully crafted to present idealized versions of reality. Scrolling through endless feeds flooded with picture-perfect images and highlight reels can create a distorted perception of life, leading to feelings of inadequacy and self-doubt. The constant pressure to match these unrealistic standards can erode self-esteem and contribute to pervasive dissatisfaction with one's life.

Moreover, social media fosters a culture of comparison unlike any other. With the ability to glimpse into the lives of others at any moment, users often find themselves caught in a perpetual cycle of comparison; they constantly evaluate their achievements, appearances, and experiences against those of their peers. This constant comparison not only fuels feelings of envy and resentment but also undermines people's sense of self-worth, perpetuating a cycle of negative emotions that can spiral into anxiety, depression, and other mental health disorders.

In addition to comparison, online interactions on social media can exacerbate mental health issues. The anonymity and detachment afforded by the digital realm can encourage individuals to engage in behaviors they would never consider in face-to-face interactions. Cyberbullying, doxing, hate speech, shaming, cyberstalking, trolling, and many other forms of online harassment have become rampant, with victims left vulnerable to psychological harm and trauma. The prevalence of negative interactions and toxic discourse on social media can contribute to feelings of isolation, anger, loneliness, alienation, and despair, further compromising people's mental well-being.

Furthermore, the addictive nature of social media poses a significant challenge to mental health. The dopamine-driven reward system inherent in these platforms keeps users hooked. They endlessly seek validation and approval through likes, follows, comments, and shares. This constant need for validation can create a dependency on social media, leading to compulsive usage and feelings of anxiety or withdrawal when offline.

Who is the Prettiest of Them All?

Physical Appearance & Beauty Standards

In the digital world of social media, the quest for beauty and perfection has reached unprecedented heights. With the rise of platforms like Instagram and TikTok, where visual content reigns supreme, users are bombarded with images of flawless faces, sculpted bodies, and glamorous lifestyles. Beauty is not just celebrated in this virtual world—it is also commodified, quantified, and curated perfectly. The pressure to conform to these narrow beauty standards can have profound consequences on mental health, particularly for impressionable young users. From a young age, individuals are inundated with images of airbrushed models, content creators, and influencers, setting unrealistic expectations for beauty and perpetuating an unattainable ideal. This constant exposure to idealized images can breed feelings of inadequacy, insecurity, and low self-esteem as users compare themselves unfavorably to the seemingly perfect appearances of others.

Social media's focus on physical appearance can exacerbate issues of body image dissatisfaction and eating disorders. With filters and editing tools readily available, users can manipulate their appearances to conform to societal beauty standards, further distorting perceptions of reality. The pressure to maintain a flawless image online can lead to obsessive behaviors, such as excessive exercising, restrictive eating, or even dangerous cosmetic procedures, as individuals strive to attain an unattainable level of perfection.

Additionally, the culture of comparison perpetuated by social media amplifies feelings of self-consciousness and inadequacy. Users constantly scrutinize their appearance compared to the seemingly flawless images presented by others, leading to a distorted perception of self and reinforcing a negative body image. This cycle of comparison and self-criticism can take a toll on mental well-being, contributing to feelings of depression, anxiety, and disordered eating patterns.

Furthermore, social media's emphasis on physical appearance can fuel unhealthy competition and jealousy among users. Pursuing likes, followers, and validation based on external appearance creates a hyper-competitive environment where individuals vie for attention and approval. This relentless pursuit of social validation can lead to insecurity, resentment, and even hostility toward others perceived as more attractive or successful.

Excessive use of social media platforms can lead to increased social comparisons, decreased self-presentation and sense of belonging, disordered view of one's self-image, lower self-esteem, and even instances of disordered eating (Faelens et al., 2021). Frequent posting, commenting, and viewing other's activities that relates to items of social desire and popularity can increase people's depressive symptoms and psychological distress due to comparison, seeking excessive social support and acceptance and focusing overly on their appearance and self-presentation.

It is true that although self-presentation on social media such as Instagram tends to be mostly accurate, there is a tendency to share mainly positive life events and situations, which can result in displaying an inaccurate representation of one's life (Faelens et al., 2021). Most content on Instagram tends to be selectively presented and carefully manicured to meet the expectations of social media standards. Social comparisons are a common issue when others determine their levels of success and happiness based on the presentation of others online, which can lead to many negative self- and body evaluations.

Filter Culture & Unrealistic Expectations

The pervasive influence of *filter culture* has profoundly altered societal perceptions of beauty, success, and happiness, ushering in an era fraught with unrealistic expectations. Filter culture, characterized by the widespread use of digital filters, editing tools, and curated content on social media platforms, creates a facade of flawlessness and perfection. From edited selfies to meticulously curated vacation snapshots, these filters and editing techniques have permeated the digital world, constructing an illusion of often unattainable perfection. This prevalence of filter culture on social media platforms poses grave implications for individuals' self-esteem, body image, and overall mental well-being. Filter culture fuels users' feelings of inadequacy, comparison, and self-doubt by perpetuating unattainable beauty standards and lifestyle ideals. The constant exposure to meticulously curated content featuring flawless faces, sculpted bodies, and opulent lifestyles distorts reality, leading individuals to measure their worth against impossible standards, inevitably feeling a sense of lack.

Filter culture fosters perfectionism and performance, where individuals are pressured to present immaculate and curated versions of themselves to the world. This relentless pursuit of a flawless online persona can be draining and anxiety-inducing as individuals grapple with the pressure to live up to the unattainable expectations of filtered images and newsfeeds. The fear of criticism for imperfections perpetuates a cycle of self-censorship and insecurity as individuals strive to reconcile their authentic selves with the idealized versions portrayed on social media. Filter culture exacerbates preexisting mental health issues, such as anxiety, depression, and body dysmorphia, as individuals internalize unrealistic beauty standards and lifestyle ideals propagated on social media. The constant thirst for perfection and validation through likes, comments, and followers exacts a toll on individuals' mental and emotional well-being. Therefore, feelings of worthlessness, isolation, and disconnection from reality are heightened.

The pervasive influence of filter culture on social media platforms underscores a troubling trend toward unrealistic expectations and ideals. By perpetuating a culture of perfectionism and comparison, filter culture exacerbates feelings of inadequacy and insecurity among users, posing significant threats to mental well-being. Urgent action is needed to challenge and mitigate the harmful effects of filter culture, promoting authenticity, self-compassion, and acceptance in this digital age.

Surveillance & Privacy

Social media dominates the digital era, and the pervasive surveillance and erosion of privacy have become pressing concerns, casting a shadow over the once-celebrated promise of connectivity and information exchange. As users innocently share their thoughts, experiences, and personal details online, they unknowingly surrender control over their digital identities to the platforms they frequent. Behind the guise of targeted advertising and personalized content lies a sinister reality: the constant monitoring and analysis of users' behaviors, preferences, and interactions. Social media companies, driven by profit motives and data hunger, harvest vast amounts of personal information, constructing digital profiles that paint an alarmingly accurate picture of individuals' lives.

The consequences of this surveillance state extend far beyond the realm of targeted ads and algorithmic recommendations. The erosion of privacy in the digital sphere has profound implications for individuals' autonomy, security, and mental well-being. Users relinquish a piece of their privacy with every click, like, and share, unwittingly exposing themselves to many risks.

From identity theft and online harassment to data breaches and surveillance capitalism, the digital world is fraught with peril, leaving individuals vulnerable and exposed. This relentless scrutiny and commodification of personal data have far-reaching effects on individuals' psyches, instilling a pervasive sense of anxiety, distrust, and vulnerability. The constant awareness of being watched and analyzed breeds a culture of self-censorship and paranoia as individuals view the digital realm with trepidation, mindful of the ever-watchful eyes of unseen algorithms and data brokers. Moreover, the erosion of privacy undermines trust and social cohesion as users realize that their most intimate moments and thoughts are no longer their own.

As we confront the unsettling reality of pervasive surveillance and eroding privacy in the digital age, it is crucial to acknowledge its profound impact on individuals' lives. Privacy erosion not only threatens our fundamental rights and freedoms but also exacts a toll on our mental and emotional well-being. As we learn about the complex terrain of social media and digital connectivity, we must advocate for greater transparency, accountability, and regulatory oversight to safeguard our privacy rights and preserve our autonomy in an increasingly surveilled world.

Video Games & Doomsday Scenarios

Impact of Video Games & Their Potential to Cause Mental Turmoil

Although video games offer an irresistible escape from reality and an opportunity to explore fantastical worlds and scenarios, they also come with psychological considerations. Video games can evoke intense emotional responses. They may contribute to mental turmoil in players, particularly in the realm of doomsday narratives and postapocalyptic settings.

The immersive nature of video games blurs the line between fiction and reality, often leading players to become deeply invested in the virtual worlds they inhabit. As players go through apocalypses and confront existential threats, they may experience heightened levels of stress, anxiety, and existential dread. The looming specter of global catastrophe, presented in vivid detail through stunning visuals and compelling storytelling, can trigger a visceral response in players, leaving them feeling overwhelmed and helpless in the face of impending doom.

Glorifying violence and destruction in some video games can desensitize players to the gravity of real-world threats. In postapocalyptic settings, where survival often hinges on combat and confrontation, players may become desensitized to the consequences of violence, viewing it as a necessary means to an end. This normalization of violence can foster a sense of detachment from the real-world implications of aggression and conflict, leading to a desensitization that undermines efforts to address pressing global challenges, such as war, environmental degradation, and social inequality.

The immersive nature of video games can foster a sense of nihilism and hopelessness in players, particularly when confronted with the inevitability of a doomsday scenario. As players grapple with the existential themes of death, decay, and despair, they may internalize a sense of futility and resignation, questioning the meaning and purpose of their actions in a world on the brink of collapse. This existential angst can contribute to feelings of alienation, isolation, and existential crisis, exacerbating mental health issues, such as depression, anxiety, and existential dread.

Doomsday: A Mainstream Weapon

Doomsday scenarios, as depicted in shows, movies, and games, offer audiences a glimpse into postapocalyptic worlds ravaged by catastrophe and chaos. From nuclear Armageddon to viral outbreaks and environmental collapse, these narratives explore the darkest corners of human imagination, portraying a world on the brink of collapse due to humanity's inherent greed and outlandish desires. Through vivid imagery and compelling storytelling, these works of fiction serve as cautionary tales, warning of the consequences of unchecked ambition, exploitation, and environmental degradation.

In recent years, doomsday scenarios have become increasingly prevalent in mainstream media and social media platforms, where sensationalist headlines and fear-inducing narratives are abound. Influencers, pundits, and media personalities often leverage these narratives to invoke fear in their audiences, capitalizing on the inherent human fascination with catastrophe and the unknown. This exploitation of fear serves to fragment and polarize societies, as individuals are bombarded with messages of doom and despair, leading to heightened anxiety, mistrust, and division within communities. The proliferation of doomsday scenarios in media contributes to a sense of apathy and resignation among audiences, providing a belief that humanity is beyond redemption and that societal collapse is inevitable. This defeatist mindset erodes hope and undermines efforts to address pressing global challenges like climate change, inequality, and social injustice.

As we go through an increasingly complex and uncertain world, it is essential to critically examine the impact of doomsday narratives on societal perceptions and behaviors. Although these narratives may serve as cautionary tales, they can perpetuate a sense of fatalism and helplessness, hindering efforts to enact positive change and build a more resilient and sustainable future. By implementing dialogue, critical thinking, and collective action, we can challenge the narratives of doom and despair and work toward creating a more hopeful and inclusive vision of the future.

Influencers Selling Hoaxes

The Rise of Influencer Culture

In today's digital age, influencer culture has become synonymous with social media, reshaping consumer behavior. What began as a grassroots movement of content creators sharing their passions and interests has evolved into a multibillion-dollar industry, with influencers commanding large followings and wielding significant influence over their audiences (Baumgarth et al., 2021). Across various niches such as fashion, lifestyle, beauty, and wellness, they have emerged as trusted authorities, setting trends, promoting products, perpetuating beauty standards, and prioritizing physical appearance (Lou et al., 2023). With their curated content and aspirational lifestyles, influencers showcase idealized versions of beauty, often featuring unrealistic beauty standards and overly glamourized lives watched daily by millions online.

Although influencers aim to inspire and engage their followers, the unrealistic expectations they promote through carefully scripted and edited content can cultivate the opposite effect among their audiences (Lou et al., 2023). Young people are especially prone to comparing what they see online and their reality, which can promote an epidemic of low self-esteem, body image issues, and feelings of inadequacy based on what one consumes online daily (Lou et al., 2023). This issue is ongoing and likely to evolve as more brands, marketers, and influencers continue to shape the face of content that we consume in an increasingly digital world (Baumgarth et al., 2021).

Arbiters of Beauty

Influencers occupy a central role within beauty as arbiters of taste and style. They showcase the latest beauty trends, products, and techniques through their curated content and aspirational lifestyles, often presenting an idealized version of beauty that resonates with their followers. From flawless makeup tutorials to skincare routines and haircare tips, influencers offer a glimpse into beauty and inspire their audiences to emulate their looks and lifestyles.

Setting Unrealistic Standards

Influencers often serve as beacons of inspiration and aspiration, captivating audiences with curated content that meticulously crafts and perpetuates idealized beauty standards. Through meticulously curated images and videos, influencers present aspirational visions of beauty characterized by filter-like faces, unrealistic bodies, and lavish lifestyles, a portrayal often unattainable to the average individual. This constant exposure to elevated beauty ideals can distort reality for impressionable audiences, particularly young people, giving rise to feelings of inadequacy, insecurity, and self-doubt as they strive to meet unattainable standards.

Despite the intention of influencers to inspire and engage their followers, the unintended consequence of perpetuating unrealistic beauty standards can have detrimental effects on self-esteem and mental well-being, exposing the intricate and nuanced dynamics within the world of influencers. Society is grappling with the impact of influencer culture on perceptions of beauty and self-worth. Therefore, it becomes increasingly vital to critically examine the content disseminated by influencers and its broader implications for individual and societal well-being.

The Impact on Self-Perception

The relentless pursuit of beauty ideals perpetuated by influencers profoundly impacts their followers' self-perceptions and mental well-being. Individuals are inundated with curated content showcasing flawless images of influencers, portraying an idealized version of beauty that seems unattainable to the average person. This constant exposure to such elevated beauty standards can harm individuals' self-esteem and body image. As they compare themselves to the seemingly perfect images presented by influencers, feelings of inadequacy and low self-esteem can arise as individuals strive to achieve an unrealistic level of perfection. The pressure to conform to these unattainable beauty standards creates a sense of perpetual dissatisfaction with one's appearance, fueling a cycle of negative self-talk and self-criticism. Constantly striving to meet the unrealistic standards of influencers can create immense pressure and anxiety, particularly among those who feel they do not align with the influencer's idealized image of beauty. This heightened sense of stress and anxiety can lead to a deterioration in mental well-being as individuals grapple with feelings of inadequacy and self-doubt. In severe cases, the pressure to conform to these beauty standards can contribute to the development or exacerbation of mental health conditions, such as depression and anxiety disorders.

The pervasiveness of influencers on social media platforms amplifies the impact of these beauty ideals on individuals' mental well-being. With constant access to curated content on social media feeds, individuals are bombarded with images of perfection, creating an unrealistic standard to which they must adhere. This constant exposure to idealized beauty can intensify feelings of inadequacy and self-doubt as individuals internalize these unattainable standards and struggle to reconcile them with their appearance. As a result, the pursuit of beauty ideals promoted by influencers can have far-reaching consequences on individuals' mental health, perpetuating a cycle of dissatisfaction and self-criticism that undermines their overall well-being.

Rumors & Rhetoric

The rapid dissemination of information and proliferation of social media platforms have given rise to a new era of rumors and rhetoric. The instantaneous nature of social media causes rumors to spread like wildfire, often fueling fear, uncertainty, and division within communities. Whether unfounded conspiracy theories, malicious gossip, or sensationalist headlines, rumors can shape perceptions, incite emotions, and perpetuate falsehoods with far-reaching consequences.

The prevalence of rumors and rhetoric on social media poses significant challenges for individuals and society. In an environment where misinformation and disinformation abound, distinguishing fact from fiction becomes increasingly complex, leading to confusion, mistrust, and polarization. Moreover, the viral nature of rumors on social media can amplify their impact, reaching a broad audience and shaping public discourse on important issues.

The spread of rumors and rhetoric on social media can also have profound effects on individuals' mental health and well-being. Exposure to sensationalist content, false narratives, and inflammatory rhetoric can trigger feelings of anxiety, anger, and distress as individuals grapple with the uncertainty and unpredictability of the information. Moreover, the echo chambers and filter bubbles that characterize social media can reinforce existing biases and beliefs, exacerbating feelings of alienation, frustration, and anger among marginalized or misunderstood users. Spreading rumors and rhetoric on social media can erode trust in institutions, furthering societal divisions and undermining efforts to foster dialogue and cooperation. When misinformation and sensationalism dominate public discourse, meaningful engagement and collaboration become increasingly challenging, hindering progress on important social, political, and economic issues.

The prevalence of rumors and rhetoric on social media underscores the importance of critical thinking, media literacy, and responsible digital citizenship. By cultivating a healthy skepticism toward sensationalist content, engaging in constructive dialogue, and verifying information before sharing, individuals can help mitigate the spread of rumors and rhetoric and promote a more informed and resilient society. Society can also bridge divides and build a more inclusive and cohesive digital community by implementing empathy, understanding, and respect for diverse perspectives.

Chapter 4

Unraveling Tensions – Immigrants

American Immigrants

In the swirling cauldron of societal discord, few groups bear the brunt of anguish and apprehension as profoundly as immigrants. Within the blend of immigrant experiences, the plight of American immigrants unfolds as a harrowing tale of systemic injustices. These injustices are interwoven with the fabric of mental illness, such as anger and anxiety.

Although this chapter focuses on immigrants, it is essential to recognize and respect the diversity regarding the terms Black Americans and African Americans, which are often used interchangeably. However, these terms can have different connotations and refer to different groups within the broader Black community in the U.S. For Black Americans, the struggle is twofold—grappling with the weight of historical trauma and contending with the relentless tide of contemporary prejudice. From the shadows of slavery to the scars of segregation, the journey toward equality has been marred by obstacles at every turn. The annals of history tell a grim tale of exploitation and oppression, as Black Americans have endured centuries of exploitation and marginalization.

Despite strides toward progress, the echoes of racial discrimination reverberate through the corridors of time, leaving behind a legacy of unresolved tensions that continue to shape reality today. The legacy of slavery casts a long shadow over the Black American community, haunting its collective memory and shaping lived experiences. From the auction block to the cotton fields, the horrors of slavery left an indelible mark on the Black American psyche, instilling a deep-seated sense of fear and mistrust. The trauma of bondage is not easily forgotten as generations of Black Americans continue to grapple with the intergenerational scars of their ancestors.

The immigration of Black individuals to the U.S. has been a substantial part of the American reality throughout the 20th century. However, the number of immigrants from the Caribbean islands increased significantly since 1965 (Maddox, 2022). Miami and New York City became the major immigration destinations for Black immigrants, with 25% of the Black population in New York City being foreign-born (Waters, 2022). Despite a significant portion of the American population being Black, pluralistic values exist toward race, identity, and culture.

For many Blacks who immigrated to the U.S. during the 1990s, the situation was different, with many choosing to adopt a monolithic American culture. Nowadays, the variety of cultures in the country leans toward greater adoption of one's racial and ethnic identity. Many Black immigrants continue to struggle to adopt the American identity even after receiving citizenship and lean toward their cultural heritage. Even Black Americans, individuals born in the U.S., struggle to adopt the entire American culture, especially when paired with the ongoing societal segregation and division.

In the aftermath of emancipation, the promise of freedom was an elusive dream for many Black Americans. The specter of Jim Crow loomed large, ushering in an era of segregation and discrimination that denied Blacks a culture of rights and dignity. From the brutality of lynchings to the indignity of separate but equal, Black Americans faced violence and injustice at every turn. The struggle for civil rights became a rallying cry for equality and justice as activists and advocates fought tirelessly to dismantle the pillars of White supremacy.

African American immigrants find themselves at a unique intersection of identity and belonging. For many, the search for acceptance is fraught with challenges as they deal with the murky waters of cultural assimilation while preserving the essence of their heritage. Caught between the allure of integration and the pull of ancestral roots, they are forced to confront the duality of their existence, grappling with the burden of straddling two worlds.

The African American immigrant experience is an intricate narrative woven with strands of resistance. From the African continent to the streets of America, they carry their forefathers' heritage while traversing the dangerous seas of identity and belonging. Treading the divide between their African roots and American realities, they grapple with the weight of dual identities, torn between the allure of assimilation and pull of cultural heritage. Despite their challenges, African Americans persevere, drawing strength from their rich cultural heritages and resilient spirit. Their narratives are of tenacity in the face of hardship, demonstrating the power of perseverance and hope.

Global Community

Beyond the shores of America, similar narratives of anguish and disquiet unfold across the globe. From the crowded streets of bustling metropolises to the desolate sceneries of refugee camps, immigrants find themselves trapped in a web of uncertainty and insecurity. Fleeing war-torn homelands or seeking refuge from political persecution, they embark on perilous journeys in search of sanctuary and solace. Nevertheless, the promise of a better life often remains elusive as they encounter barriers erected by xenophobia and prejudice. From discriminatory immigration policies to hostile societal attitudes, the path to integration is fraught with obstacles, leaving immigrants trapped in a cycle of despair and disillusionment. With each passing day, the weight of uncertainty grows heavier, casting a shadow over their hopes and aspirations.

The number of asylum seekers and refugees around the world has grown dramatically due to growing tensions and conflicts. In the U.S. alone, the number of individuals seeking refuge increased 74% between 2015 and 2017 (Donato & Ferris, 2020). Since 2017, the number of refugees has decreased to 32,000 in 2019 from 54,000 in 2017. For a large part of American history, refugees and migrants were not considered as distinct groups of individuals fleeing war as opposed to seeking labor opportunities. This view changed in the 1930s when the High Commissioners and the League of Nations established the difference between the two groups. This fruition resulted in establishing the United Nations (UN) High Commissioner for Refugees in 1950 and the Convention Related to the Status of the Refugees in 1951. Nowadays, the refugee concept is an established legal term recognized by American and international jurisprudence.

As the world grapples with the complexities of immigration, it is imperative to recognize the human cost of indifference and apathy. Behind the headlines and statistics lie stories of grit as immigrants experience the treacherous terrain of displacement and upheaval. These stories are testaments to the indomitable spirit of the human soul; they serve as reminders that hope endures amidst the chaos and turmoil. In the face of mounting tensions and uncertainty, it is crucial to extend a hand of compassion and solidarity to those who find themselves on the fringes of society. With an environment of inclusivity and acceptance, we can pave the way toward a brighter future where the bonds of empathy and understanding replace the shackles of prejudice.

The Search for a Place to Belong

Within the intricate labyrinth of immigrant experiences, individuals from diverse backgrounds embark on poignant quests for belonging amidst the shifting sands of identity and cultural heritage. For many, searching for a place to call home is not just a physical journey but also a profound odyssey through the tangled web of history and memory.

Rooted in their ancestral lands yet displaced by globalization and conflict, immigrants grapple with the complexities of identity and heritage. The search for belonging is a soul-stirring endeavor, a spiritual quest to reclaim their roots and lost heritage. From the haunting melodies of traditional music to the comforting aromas of home-cooked meals, they seek solace in the echoes of their past, forging connections to their cultural heritage that transcend the boundaries of time and space.

The unique challenge of moving to a new country, whether by seeking refuge or labor, is preserving one's unique cultural identity and heritage while adapting to the new country. The main issue for many migrants is language maintenance; for many cultures, their language is a source of heritage capital and a distinction for various diasporic populations worldwide (Maddox, 2022). For many, language remains a tool for communicating with the family and a source of ethnic identity. Immigrant children often bear the tension of identifying with their heritage and their new country, especially those who hold an ethnicity different from that in their new country (Maddox, 2022). Although it is clear that many first-generation immigrants develop their sense of identity and heritage around adolescence, the acculturation and identity adaptation process of adult immigrants becomes more challenging to understand.

Nevertheless, the journey toward belonging is fraught with formidable obstacles as immigrants face the treacherous terrain of racism, xenophobia, and discrimination. The specter of prejudice casts a long shadow, obscuring the path to acceptance and thwarting the realization of their aspirations and dreams. From discriminatory immigration policies to social marginalization, immigrants confront systemic barriers that undermine their sense of belonging and deny them access to the full rights and privileges of citizenship.

Immigrants remain resolute and unhinged despite challenges, drawing strength from their shared history and collective struggles. Their quest for belonging is a stirring testament to the indomitable human spirit, a defiant assertion of their right to exist and thrive in a world that often seeks to erase their presence. In their search for a place to belong, they cultivate communities, erecting bridges of solidarity that span continents and cultures.

The search for belonging transcends the individual realm, evolving into a collective endeavor to forge a world that celebrates diversity and inclusivity. This search serves as a poignant reminder that true belonging knows no boundaries of race, nationality, or ethnicity, embracing the kaleidoscope of human experience in all its vibrant hues. As immigrants continue their relentless pursuit of a place to belong, they inspire us all to strive for a society where everyone is seen, heard, and valued for their intrinsic worth and unique contributions. The quest for belonging emerges as a timeless narrative, weaving together the hopes, struggles, and triumphs of past, present, and future generations. It is a voyage characterized by unity and unwavering resolve. This journey ultimately unveils the truth: within the expansive fabric of humanity, we are all interconnected and linked by the common thread of our shared humanity.

War & Famine: The Mental Turmoil of Desperate Exodus

As immigrants begin their journeys to escape the horrors of war and famine, they are not only confronted with physical dangers but also endure profound mental and emotional struggles. The decision to leave behind everything familiar and embark on a journey into the unknown is fraught with uncertainty and fear, leaving deep scars on the psyche. For many, the harrowing experiences of war and famine leave indelible imprints on their mental well-being, haunting their thoughts and dreams long after they have fled to safety. The trauma of witnessing violence, loss, and deprivation inflicts deep wounds, triggering a cascade of psychological distress that reverberates through their lives.

In many cases, refugees and asylum seekers escaping war suffer from various mental and physical strains due to exposure to traumatic and violent experiences in their home countries. Many develop post-traumatic stress disorder (PTSD), a disorder that can make it more challenging to adapt to a new culture and country as a result of the psychological wounds and distress experienced (Tineo et al., 2021). Many refugees have experienced a loss of home, not just in the physical sense but also emotionally, due to the loss of family members from war or conflict (Tineo et al., 2021). War can lead to existential disturbances where surviving family members question their existence in light of death or suffering experienced by others in their countries (Tineo et al., 2021). Traumatic dissociation can occur among those who continue to question their right to existence and develop a syndrome of homelessness even after settling in a new place (Tineo et al., 2021). The horrors of war are etched into the fabric of their being, leaving them grappling with nightmares and flashbacks that refuse to fade with time. The sound of explosions, the sight of bloodshed, the smell of burning flesh—these are the memories that haunt their waking hours, leaving them trembling with fear and uncertainty.

Similarly, the specter of famine casts a long shadow over their minds as they recall the gnawing hunger, the desperate search for food, and the agony of watching loved ones waste away before their eyes. The trauma of starvation leaves them haunted by a profound sense of helplessness and despair as they struggle to make sense of a world torn apart by hunger and deprivation. As they flee their war-torn homelands or famine-stricken regions, immigrants are confronted with a myriad of challenges that exacerbate their mental anguish. The constant threat of violence, the uncertainty of their future, and the anguish of leaving loved ones behind weigh heavily on their minds, fueling feelings of anxiety, depression, and despair. The journey is fraught with peril as immigrants endure treacherous routes, grueling conditions, and the constant threat of exploitation and abuse. The physical toll of the journey is matched only by the psychological toll as they grapple with the constant fear of danger and the anguish of uncertainty.

Even after reaching their destinations, the mental struggles persist as immigrants confront the challenges of adjusting to a new life in a foreign land. The cultural shock, the language barrier, and the struggle to find employment and housing further exacerbate their mental anguish, leaving them feeling isolated, disoriented, and alone. It is common for immigrants to experience a profound sense of hopelessness and despair as they grapple with the enormity of their trauma and the uncertainty of their future. The scars of war and famine run deep, leaving lasting scars on their hearts and minds that cannot be easily healed.

Nevertheless, amidst the darkness, there is also strength. Immigrants draw on the power of community, faith, and inner fortitude to persevere in difficulties. They find solace in the bonds of solidarity forged with fellow travelers, the acts of kindness extended by strangers, and the hope of building a better future for themselves and their loved ones. Therefore, the journey of fleeing war and famine is not just a physical passage but also a profound odyssey of the soul, marked by struggle and, ultimately, the triumph of the human spirit. As immigrants face the treacherous waters of displacement and upheaval, they remind us of the enduring power of hope, determination, and the indomitable human spirit.

Integration & Racism

Cultural Adaptation & Discrimination

For immigrants, the journey toward integration into a new society is often fraught with obstacles, and the pervasive specter of racism. As they strive to carve out a place for themselves in their adopted homeland, immigrants grapple with the dual challenges of preserving their cultural identity while dealing with the complexities of assimilation. Racism, in its myriad forms, casts a long shadow over the immigrant experience. It manifests in overt discrimination, systemic barriers, and microaggressions that chip away at immigrants' sense of belonging. From exclusionary immigration policies to hostile encounters in their daily lives, immigrants are confronted with a constant barrage of reminders that they are viewed as outsiders, unwelcome in their newfound communities.

In light of greater global internationalization, cultural and cross-cultural adaptation became important concepts for immigrants. Many immigrants continue to experience obstacles related to culture shock, language barriers, homesickness, and loneliness in the new country, which is further reinforced by discrimination in the new country (Waters, 2022). Waters (2022) linked perceived discrimination against immigrants to several psychological problems that are detrimental to their ability or willingness to adapt culturally to the new country. Adaptation difficulties can be additionally complicated by struggling to understand the new country's social norms, values, and customs (Waters, 2022). The process of cross-cultural adaptation typically consists of psychological and sociocultural adaptation; the immigrant develops social skills that allow them to interact successfully with individuals from the host country while improving their life satisfaction, self-esteem, and well-being.

The struggle for integration is further compounded by the insidious nature of structural racism, from housing and employment to education and healthcare. Immigrants often find themselves relegated to the margins, denied access to opportunities and resources that are readily available to their native-born counterparts. Nevertheless, despite the pervasive challenges they face, immigrants remain resilient. They draw strength from their cultural heritage and community bonds, forging networks of support that serve as bulwarks against the tide of prejudice. Through grassroots activism, advocacy, and collective action, immigrants and their allies work tirelessly to dismantle the barriers of racism and create more inclusive and equitable societies.

The fight against racism is not merely a struggle for immigrants; rights; it is also a battle for the soul of society itself. It is a call to confront the uncomfortable truths of our shared history, acknowledge the deep-seated inequalities that continue to shape our present, and envision a future where every individual is valued and respected regardless of race, ethnicity, or immigration status.

Verbal & Physical Abuse

Confronting Violence in Search of Stability

For immigrants, the journey toward integration is often marred by the harsh realities of verbal and physical abuse. These forms of violence, whether overt or subtle, serve as painful reminders of the hostility and prejudice they encounter in their new environments. Verbal abuse takes many forms, from derogatory slurs and xenophobic remarks to microaggressions and bullying. Immigrants are subjected to demeaning language that undermines their dignity and sense of belonging, eroding their confidence and self-worth. Such verbal assaults can have profound psychological effects, leaving lasting scars on the psyche of the individual and the community.

Moreover, physical abuse is a grim reality for many immigrants who face the threat of violence in their daily lives. From hate crimes and assaults to domestic violence and workplace abuse, immigrants are vulnerable to physical harm at the hands of perpetrators fueled by bigotry and intolerance. These acts of violence not only inflict physical pain but also instill fear and trauma, disrupting their efforts to build stable and secure lives. Despite their challenges, immigrants demonstrate remarkable power. They draw strength from their communities, banding together to support one another and resist oppression. Grassroots organizations and advocacy groups provide vital resources and assistance to those affected by verbal and physical abuse, empowering them to assert their rights and demand justice.

With the growing number of supporters of anti-immigration and racist policies and leaders, the mass media continue to portray discrimination and hostility toward immigrants negatively (March, 2020). As a result, hostile media rhetoric about immigrants and refugees leads to greater verbal and physical abuse and lower prosociality in interactions with immigrants. Favoritism in society develops, creating a broader social divide and lower ethnic homogeneity. Anti-immigration sentiments start to develop, increasing feelings of threat and alienation toward immigrants and worsening the intergroup relations among members of society.

Prolonged negativity toward immigrants can lead to zero ethnic diversity and reduced intergroup interactions. Therefore, in the fight against verbal and physical abuse, allies play a crucial role in amplifying immigrant voices and challenging systemic injustices. By standing in solidarity with immigrants, advocating for policy changes, and promoting cultural understanding and acceptance, we can work toward creating safer and more inclusive communities for all.

Women & Children: Vulnerabilities Amidst Migration

Within the chaos of immigration, women and children emerge as particularly vulnerable populations. They face unique challenges and hardships as they try to understand the complexities of migration and integration. For women, the journey of immigration is often fraught with peril as they confront heightened risks of exploitation, abuse, and discrimination. Many women find themselves exposed to gender-based violence, including sexual assault, trafficking, and domestic abuse, both during their journeys and after arriving in their new countries. The pervasive threat of violence looms large, casting a shadow over their efforts to build stable and secure lives for themselves and their families.

Worldwide displacement due to war and conflict is a significant cause of health determinants and death of women and children. Amodu et al. (2020) estimated that displacement is responsible for 60% of preventable deaths among women, 53% of deaths among under-5-year-olds, and 45% of natal deaths. Women and children are the highest population of displaced people around the world. When fleeing with children, women often face challenges in accessing healthcare due to trauma and wounds, which are attributed to the premature death rates. Many displaced pregnant women suffer complications during pregnancy, unattended childbirths, and unplanned pregnancies.

Although humanitarian organizations try to provide support for women fleeing their countries with children, they cannot provide the same level of protection to all women in need. International policies have disproportionately targeted the health and well-being of refugees in developed countries. In addition, much less such support is provided to women and children fleeing war-ridden countries. As long as women and children remain within the borders of their home countries, they are subject to the protection of that government, which is often why these women and children do not receive the support that they need.

Moreover, children bear the brunt of the immigrant experience, grappling with the upheaval and uncertainty that accompany displacement. Forced to leave behind familiar surroundings and support networks, immigrant children face profound challenges in adapting to their new environments. Language barriers, cultural differences, and limited access to education and healthcare further compound their struggles, leaving them vulnerable to exploitation and neglect. Moreover, immigrant women and children are disproportionately affected by poverty and social exclusion due to the lack of support systems that are often ill-equipped to meet their unique needs. Discriminatory policies and inadequate support services leave many immigrant families on the margins, struggling to access essential resources and opportunities for advancement.

Every immigrant has a strong sense of cultural heritage and resilience. Many leave their countries behind in response to conflict and war and embark on a journey of adaptation, solace, and numerous barriers. The struggles of discrimination, racism, and xenophobia make it challenging for many to settle and adapt to the new identity. The integration journey for many remains harsh and complex in light of the obstacles of abuse, prejudice, and hostility in the new country. For many, the journey is more complex than for others due to the unique challenges associated with language, race, and religion in the new country.

Chapter 5

Unraveling Tensions – Black Americans

The term *Black American* in this chapter refers to anyone of the Black race who is born in America. This term can include descendants of the Caribbean islands or Africa. On the other hand, *African Americans* are individuals born on the African continent who have received American citizenship. In contrast, *Africans* are immigrants from the African continent who have not been born in the U.S. and do not have American citizenship (Belgrave & Allison, 2018). This chapter will focus on Black Americans, individuals of the Black race born or with citizenship in the U.S.

As we dive deeper into the many layers of rage, anxiety, and other mental health challenges the Black American community faces, find themselves in a situation plagued with deep-seated fears and profound apprehensions. This exploration calls for a nuanced understanding of the profound impact of systemic injustices, persistent discrimination, and the enduring scars of historical trauma etched into the collective consciousness. For generations, Black Americans have borne the heavy burden of inequality and systemic oppression, contending with a relentless onslaught of racial discrimination, economic disparities, and the pervasive specter of violence. These persistent adversities carve deep into the psyche, creating an environment where anger and anxiety become almost inevitable responses to the constant threat of injustice and marginalization.

As we dive under the surface of the Black American experience, we see an intricate pattern woven with strands of tenacity and grit, but tainted by the persistent legacy of racial trauma and systemic injustice. The weight of intergenerational trauma, stemming from centuries of slavery, segregation, and institutionalized racism, casts a long shadow over the community, thus perpetuating cycles of anger, despair, and emotional turmoil. In recent years, heightened awareness of police violence against Black individuals has sparked waves of righteous indignation and collective unrest. The tragic deaths of George Floyd, Breonna Taylor, and countless others serve as stark reminders of the systemic devaluation of Black lives and the urgent need for substantive societal changes.

Moreover, the COVID-19 pandemic has barred and exacerbated existing disparities within Black communities, amplifying economic hardship, healthcare inequities, and the profound trauma of loss. These compounding challenges have intensified feelings of fear, isolation, and despair, further magnifying the already precarious state of mental well-being. People's complexity requires acknowledging and dismantling the structural barriers perpetuating systemic inequality and disenfranchisement. It demands a collective reckoning with the entrenched forces of oppression that continue to undermine the dignity and well-being of Black Americans.

Society must redouble its efforts to address the root causes of anger, anxiety, and mental health struggles within the Black community. This process entails not only addressing immediate needs for mental health support and resources but also enacting substantive policy changes aimed at dismantling systems of oppression and resulting in a more equitable society. Ultimately, unraveling the Black American community's tensions necessitates a multifaceted approach centered on justice, equity, and collective healing. Only through concerted efforts to confront systemic inequities and foster environments of genuine care and support can we hope to mitigate the profound toll of anger, anxiety, and mental health challenges on Black lives.

Disbelief & Heartbreak

When we discuss the experiences of Black Americans, the emotions of disbelief and heartbreak weave deeply into their everyday lives. These emotions stem from a complex interplay of historical injustices, ongoing systemic racism, and personal encounters with discrimination and violence.

Disbelief permeates the collective consciousness of the Black community as they bear witness to the persistent injustices that plague their lives. Despite promises of progress and equality, the reality on the ground often tells a starkly different story. Time and again, Black Americans find themselves confronted with instances of racial profiling, police brutality, and institutionalized discrimination, leading to a profound sense of disillusionment with the justice system and society at large.

Heartbreak accompanies each news report of another life lost to senseless violence or systemic neglect. Whether it is the tragic death of a loved one at the hands of law enforcement or the devastating toll of generational poverty and lack of access to healthcare, the pain runs deep within the Black community. Each loss serves as a painful reminder of the fragility of life and the harsh realities of living in a society that systematically devalues Black lives.

Enduring Trauma: The Heartbreak of Systemic Injustice

The trauma inflicted by the firsthand experience of injustice reverberates throughout the lives of Black Americans, leaving indelible marks on their hearts and minds that shape their daily existence in profound ways. These wounds, akin to deep scars, penetrate the essence of their being, embedding a sense of pain and disillusionment that cannot easily be erased. From the historical legacy of slavery to contemporary manifestations of racial bias and discrimination, the Black community has endured centuries of systemic oppression that have undermined their sense of safety, security, and belonging. The repeated exposure to systemic injustice not only inflicts immediate harm but also perpetuates a cycle of trauma that spans generations. The erosion of trust in institutions meant to protect all Americans, such as law enforcement and the judicial system, exacerbates feelings of vulnerability and betrayal. Despite striving to adhere to the principles of justice and equality, these institutions often fall short, perpetuating a sense of marginalization and disenfranchisement among Black individuals. This pervasive sense of vulnerability becomes a constant companion as Black individuals deal with a society that all too often denies the population humanity and ignores the population grievances.

The psychological toll of enduring systemic injustice cannot be overstated. It breeds a profound sense of powerlessness and despair as individuals grapple with the harsh reality of being targeted and marginalized simply because of the color of Black Americans' skin. Each member of the Black community carries the weight of this collective trauma, impacting their mental health and well-being in a myriad of ways. From heightened levels of stress and anxiety to feelings of anger and resentment, the emotional toll of systemic injustice is immense.

Moreover, the intergenerational transmission of trauma further compounds the challenges faced by Black Americans. The scars of past injustices, from slavery and segregation to mass incarceration and police brutality, linger in the collective memory of the community, shaping their worldview and sense of identity. The legacy of historical trauma casts a long shadow over the present, fueling feelings of disbelief and heartbreak as Black individuals confront the enduring reality of systemic racism and inequality.

The Courage of Black America

In moments of disbelief and despair, Black Americans draw strength from the profound history that is shared, marked by perseverance, power, and utmost commitment. From the shores of West Africa to the plantations of the antebellum South, from the battlefields of the Civil Rights Movement to the streets of contemporary America, Black individuals have stood shoulder to shoulder in defiance of oppression and injustice. This shared history serves as a source of strength and inspiration, a testament to the indomitable spirit of a people who have persevered in the face of unimaginable hardship. This history is marked by courage, sacrifice, and solidarity as ordinary men and women rose to challenge the status quo and demand a better future for themselves and their children.

In times of hardship, this legacy of resistance serves as a guiding light, reminding Black Americans of their inherent power and agency. It instills a sense of pride and dignity, fueling their resolve to speak truth to power and advocate for change. It is a reminder that, despite their obstacles, they are not alone; they are part of a vibrant and resilient community that has weathered countless storms and emerged stronger on the other side. This solidarity is evident in the countless grassroots movements and community organizations that have sprung up in response to systemic injustice. From Black Lives Matter to the National Association for the Advancement of Colored People, local mutual aid groups, and national advocacy organizations, Black Americans have come together to build power and effect change. They have reclaimed their narratives by amplifying the Black race voices and demanding a seat at the table in the fight for justice and equality.

This sense of community and collective purpose sustains Black Americans in their quest for dignity and liberation. Despite their challenges, it is a reminder that Black Americans are not alone; they are part of a more significant movement for social change sweeping the nation. Moreover, as Black Americans continue to stand together in solidarity, refusing to be silenced or sidelined, they have created the foundation for a more just and equitable future for all future generations.

Stereotypes and Fears

Stereotypes and fears loom large in the lived experiences of Black Americans, shaping Black individuals' interactions with the world and influencing their perceptions of themselves and others. From the pervasive stereotype of the "dangerous Black man" to the hypersexualization of Black women, these harmful tropes perpetuate a cycle of prejudice and discrimination that undermines the humanity of Black individuals. Although the world has experienced a widespread phenomenon of sexualization of the female body, leading to greater objectification and body shame, the sexualization of Black women became a lot more widespread. Predominately rooted in slavery and colonialism, the hypersexualization of Black women became more prominent as a result of hip-hop music and the greater spreading of misogynistic and degrading messages relating to Black women. They were typically portrayed as more submissive, materialistic, and lacking morals than others. These stereotypes were further reinforced by suggestive dancing in some of the most popular music videos (Otto et al., 2022).

The dangerous Black man stereotype has become all too familiar in recent times with the ever-growing public media coverage of Black man shootings and killings. Scholars have heavily studied the automatic assumption of danger when faced with a Black man; these scholars have agreed that people were more likely to assume a Black man was armed and would be more likely to shoot at them as a way of protecting themselves (March et al., 2021). People are also more likely to process specific behaviors as more aggressive when done by a Black man as opposed to a White man, and more are likely to assume that the Black man is angry based on his facial expressions (March et al., 2021). Such attitudes toward Black men and their strong association with danger have led to some deadly outcomes, such as the growing number of unjust killings of Black men by law enforcement. Some stereotypes are discussed in the following sections to understand better the factors behind such deadly outcomes.

Stereotypes Perpetuated Against the Black Community

Lazy

This stereotype falsely portrays Black Americans as lacking ambition or a strong work ethic. It ignores the systemic barriers historically hindering their economic and social progress. Many Black individuals work diligently in challenging circumstances, striving for success despite facing disproportionate obstacles or barriers. This stereotype perpetuates harmful misconceptions and undermines efforts to achieve racial equity and justice.

Violent

This harmful stereotype depicts Black Americans as inherently aggressive or prone to violence. It ignores the complex social factors that contribute to crime rates in marginalized communities. It unfairly vilifies Black individuals and perpetuates fear and mistrust. In truth, most Black Americans identify as law-abiding citizens who seek safety and security like anyone else. Addressing the root causes of violence, such as poverty and lack of opportunity, is crucial to combat this stereotype and promote understanding and empathy.

Unintelligent

The stereotype of Black Americans as intellectually inferior is deeply rooted in historical racism and serves to justify discriminatory practices. It disregards the achievements and contributions of Black scholars, scientists, and professionals throughout history. This stereotype is not only false but also harmful, as it perpetuates systemic inequalities in education and employment. Challenging this stereotype and recognizing individuals' intelligence and potential, regardless of race, is essential. Providing equal access to quality education and opportunities for intellectual growth is vital in dismantling this harmful belief.

Dangerous

The portrayal of Black Americans as inherently threatening or dangerous is a product of racial bias and media sensationalism. This stereotype contributes to the over-policing and criminalization of Black communities, leading to disproportionate rates of incarceration and violence. In reality, most Black individuals pose no threat to society and deserve to be treated with dignity and respect. Addressing this stereotype requires confronting implicit biases and advocating for fair and equitable treatment under the law.

Welfare-Dependent

This stereotype perpetuates the false narrative that Black Americans are overly reliant on government assistance and welfare programs. It overlooks the systemic barriers to economic mobility faced by many Black individuals, including limited access to quality education and employment discrimination. In truth, welfare assistance is often a lifeline for families struggling to make ends meet, regardless of race. By challenging this stereotype, society can work toward creating policies that address the root causes of poverty and promote economic opportunity for all.

Recognizing the Gravity of Fears

Racial Violence

Black Americans live with the constant fear of becoming victims of racially motivated violence. This fear stems from a long history of hate crimes, police brutality, and racially motivated attacks by individuals or groups. Every interaction with law enforcement or encounter with strangers carries the weight of this fear, leading to heightened anxiety and hypervigilance in everyday life.

Discrimination

The pervasive fear of experiencing discrimination and prejudice affects various aspects of a Black individual's life. From seeking employment to accessing housing, education, and healthcare, there is an underlying anxiety about facing barriers and unfair treatment due to race. This fear can erode trust in institutions and lead to reluctance to seek help or support when needed.

Injustice

Black individuals fear being unfairly targeted or treated within the criminal justice system. Historical and ongoing systemic racism within law enforcement and the legal system fuel this fear. The fear of being wrongly accused, being harshly sentenced, or encountering biased treatment have amplified distrust in the institutions meant to uphold justice.

Economic Insecurity

Economic instability looms large for Black Americans due to systemic barriers to employment and wealth accumulation. Limited access to quality education and resources exacerbates this fear. The persistent racial wealth gap and disparities in income and employment opportunities create a sense of vulnerability and uncertainty about financial security.

Losing Loved Ones

The fear of losing loved ones to violence, incarceration, or other consequences of systemic racism weighs heavily on Black families and communities. The constant threat of losing family members to police brutality, gun violence, or unjust imprisonment contributes to pervasive anxiety and trauma. This fear shapes daily life and decisions, influencing where to live, whom to trust, and how to understand relationships.

Social Stigma

Black individuals fear experiencing social stigma and negative stereotypes based on racial identity. The fear of being judged, marginalized, or discriminated against in social settings, workplaces, or educational environments contributes to stress and anxiety. This fear of being stereotyped or misunderstood can impact self-esteem, mental health, and overall well-being, leading to feelings of isolation and alienation.

Intergenerational Trauma

The fear of passing on trauma and hardships to future generations perpetuates cycles of inequality and struggle. The weight of historical trauma, including slavery, segregation, and systemic oppression, looms large. Black parents fear their children experiencing the same injustices and struggles they faced, leading to a deep sense of responsibility to protect and prepare the next generation.

Limited Opportunities

Black Americans fear that opportunities for success and advancement are limited due to systemic barriers and discrimination. The fear of hitting a glass ceiling or facing roadblocks in career advancement and educational attainment contributes to frustration and hopelessness. The fear of being overlooked or held back due to race persists despite striving for excellence and hard work.

Cultural Erasure

Black individuals fear the erasure of their cultural heritages and identities in the face of ongoing assimilation pressures and historical attempts to suppress Black culture. The fear of losing connection to their roots, language, traditions, and history contributes to loss and disconnection. This fear underscores the importance of preserving and celebrating Black culture and history as a source of pride.

Invisibility

Black individuals may fear being overlooked, ignored, or marginalized in society. The fear of not being seen or heard, of being dismissed or invalidated based on race, contributes to feelings of invisibility and alienation. This fear of being rendered invisible in social, political, and cultural contexts highlights the ongoing struggle for representation, recognition, and equality.

The Ongoing Struggle of Black Americans in a Biased Society

For Black Americans, a society steeped in racial bias and systemic oppression means constantly contending with the threat of being perceived through the lens of these stereotypes. The fear of being unjustly targeted by law enforcement or facing discrimination in employment and housing exacerbates feelings of vulnerability and distrust. This perpetual state of vigilance and hypervigilance takes a toll on mental well-being, fueling anxiety and exacerbating existing feelings of disbelief and heartbreak. The internalization of these stereotypes can lead to internalized racism, where individuals begin to believe and internalize the negative narratives imposed upon everyone by society. This internalized racism can manifest as self-doubt, low self-esteem, and a distorted sense of identity, further deepening the wounds of disbelief and heartbreak.

The legacy of historical trauma and systemic oppression casts a long shadow over the Black community, perpetuating a cycle of fear and mistrust that undermines efforts toward healing and reconciliation. Despite these challenges, Black Americans continue to resist and defy the stereotypes imposed upon them by reclaiming their narratives and asserting their humanity amidst difficulties.

Impact of Recent Events: George Floyd

The tragic death of George Floyd on May 25, 2020, sent seismic shock waves throughout the Black community and reverberated across the globe, serving as a stark reminder of the persistent racism and police brutality faced by Black Americans. Floyd's agonizing final moments, captured on video for the world to witness, laid bare the brutal reality of systemic injustice and ignited a wave of righteous anger and collective mourning. For Black Americans, Floyd's death was not just another statistic but a chilling symbol of the ongoing struggle for racial equality and justice. It represented the culmination of centuries of racial violence and oppression, a poignant manifestation of the systemic racism deeply ingrained within the fabric of American society. As his desperate pleas for mercy—"I can't breathe"—echoed in the collective consciousness, they served as a haunting reminder of the countless Black lives lost to police brutality and racial violence.

The visceral horror of witnessing Floyd's life slowly ebb away under the knee of a police officer sparked an unprecedented wave of protests and civil unrest across the U.S. and around the world. From Minneapolis to Melbourne, millions took to the streets to demand justice for Floyd and denounce the systemic racism and police brutality that continue to plague Black communities. Fueled by frustration and indignation, the protests became a powerful expression of solidarity and a forceful call for systemic changes.

The aftermath of Floyd's death laid bare the deep-seated fault lines of racial inequality and social injustice that divide American society. It exposed the vast disparities in the treatment of Black and White Americans within the criminal justice system and highlighted the urgent need for meaningful reform. The widespread outrage and condemnation that followed his murder forced a long-overdue reckoning with the legacy of racial violence and discrimination in the U.S., prompting a national conversation about race, policing, and the enduring legacy of White supremacy.

In the wake of Floyd's death, calls for justice reverberated far beyond the confines of the criminal justice system, permeating every aspect of American life. From corporate boardrooms to classrooms, from sports arenas to social media platforms, people of all races and backgrounds grappled with the uncomfortable truths laid bare by his killing. It sparked a moment of collective introspection and soul-searching as individuals and institutions confronted their complicity in perpetuating racial injustice and pledged to do better. The impact of George Floyd's death extended far beyond the immediate outrage and protests it sparked. It catalyzed a global movement for racial justice and equality, inspiring millions to join the fight against systemic racism and police brutality. It served as a wake-up call for those who had long disregarded the pervasive nature of racial injustice in their communities and galvanized a new generation of activists and advocates committed to creating a more just and equitable world for all. As the world continues to grapple with the legacy of

Floyd's death, his memory serves as a powerful reminder of the ongoing struggle for racial equality and the urgent need for meaningful change (Scotland et al., 2024).

The murder of George Floyd is just one of the many examples of unlawful and unfair killings of people of color by those in positions of authority. Some of the other notable victims, such as Sandra Bland, Trayvon Martin, and Tamir Rice, are just some of the known victims of the brutality of police officers in the country; these incidences sparked public outrage and numerous demonstrations (Scotland et al., 2024). The Black Lives Matter movement was a much-needed political, social, and ideological intervention that placed pressure on the world to recognize the humanity of Black people and their contributions and role within society. It is a sign of resilience and rebellion of the Black community in the face of historic oppression, a chance for them to have a voice in a society that continually diminishes them.

Coping With Collective Anguish & Trauma

The relentless cycle of racial violence and systemic oppression has inflicted deep wounds on the collective psyche of the Black community, leaving behind a legacy of anguish and trauma that reverberates through generations. From the horrors of slavery and Jim Crow segregation to the ongoing scourge of police brutality and institutional racism, Black Americans have borne the brunt of systemic injustice and intergenerational trauma. In the face of this collective anguish, many Black individuals and communities have developed coping mechanisms to truly understand the pervasive reality of racial violence and discrimination. These coping strategies range from seeking solace in faith and spirituality to finding strength in community and collective action. Engaging in activism and advocacy provides some a sense of purpose and empowerment, allowing them to channel their pain and anger into meaningful social change.

However, coping with collective trauma yields additional challenges. The constant exposure to images and stories of racial violence and injustice can retraumatize individuals and exacerbate feelings of hopelessness and despair. The lack of adequate mental health resources and culturally competent care further compounds the challenges faced by Black Americans struggling to cope with the psychological toll of racial trauma. The pervasive stigma surrounding mental health within the Black community may discourage individuals from seeking help or speaking openly about their struggles.

The legacy of historical trauma and systemic oppression has engendered a culture of silence and stoicism, where expressions of vulnerability and pain are often met with skepticism or dismissal. This reluctance to acknowledge and address mental health issues only serves to perpetuate the cycle of suffering and further isolate individuals in their time of need. Despite these challenges, many Black individuals and communities are finding ways to heal and resist the insidious effects of collective trauma. Culturally affirming healing practices, such as storytelling, art therapy, and communal rituals, allow individuals to process their experiences and reclaim their narratives. Building supportive networks and creating a sense of belonging can help people heal from trauma.

Despite their continuous suffering, Black Americans continue to take strength from their shared heritage of perseverance and resistance. They refuse to be defined by their pain and trauma, choosing instead to affirm their humanity and dignity in the face of oppression. By confronting the legacy of racial trauma head-on and supporting one another in their journey toward healing, Black communities have reclaimed their power and agency in the struggle for racial justice and liberation. Therefore, the following section discusses ways to improve their quality of life.

Ways to Improve Quality of Life Long-Term

Improving Black Americans' quality of life in the long-term requires a multifaceted approach. This approach must address the root causes of systemic inequality. The goal should be to promote holistic well-being.

Addressing Systemic Inequities

Meaningful progress toward improving the quality of life for Black Americans necessitates addressing systemic inequities. These inequities perpetuate racial disparities in education, employment, healthcare, and criminal justice. This process includes implementing policies that promote equitable access to resources and opportunities, dismantling discriminatory practices, and investing in historically marginalized and underserved communities.

Culturally Competent Mental Health Care

Ensuring access to culturally competent mental health care is essential for addressing the unique mental health needs of Black Americans. This process involves training mental health professionals to understand and effectively respond to the cultural and historical factors that shape the experiences of Black individuals and communities. Additionally, critical steps toward improving long-term mental health outcomes may entail increasing the availability of mental health resources in Black communities and reducing the stigma surrounding mental illness.

Promoting Economic Empowerment

Economic empowerment plays a crucial role in improving the quality of life for Black Americans by providing opportunities for financial stability, upward mobility, and economic independence. Empowerment may occur through creating initiatives to increase access to quality education and job training programs, expanding entrepreneurship opportunities, and addressing wealth disparities. Policies can target wealth-building initiatives and reparations.

Investing in Community Infrastructure

Community infrastructure is essential for creating safe, vibrant, and resilient communities where Black Americans can thrive. Leaders can address infrastructure by investing in affordable housing, neighborhood revitalization efforts, access to quality healthcare facilities, recreational spaces, and community-based organizations that provide essential services and support.

Promoting Social & Political Empowerment

Promoting social and political empowerment is essential for advancing the interests and well-being of Black Americans. Individuals and communities should be empowered to advocate for their rights, participate in politics, and hold elected officials accountable for addressing racial injustice and inequality issues. Additionally, promoting civic engagement, voter participation, and community organization efforts can help amplify the voices of Black Americans and drive meaningful social change.

Providing Healing

Fostering tolerance and healing is critical for Black Americans' long-term well-being in the face of persistent hardship and trauma. This process involves allowing people and groups to participate in culturally affirming healing traditions, including storytelling, art therapy, and communal rituals promoting healing and recovery. Furthermore, building supportive networks and cultivating a feeling of belonging may be critical sources of social support and solidarity during times of need.

We can improve the long-term quality of life for Black Americans while advancing racial justice and equity for all by addressing systemic inequities that perpetuate racial disparities, increasing access to culturally competent mental health care, promoting economic empowerment, investing in community infrastructure, promoting social and political empowerment, and fostering adaptability and healing.

Acknowledging Past Contributions

Acknowledging past contributions may help promote healing among Black Americans. Therefore, this section presents several Black American inventors who made significant contributions to all Americans in the past, but their achievements remain overlooked or underappreciated.

The Three-Light Traffic Signal

In 1923, Garrett Morgan patented three-light traffic signals. His design included adding a warning light to indicate that the signal would change, improving safety and efficiency in traffic control.

The Gas Mask

Garrett Morgan also invented the gas mask, which he patented in 1914. Originally designed to protect workers from inhaling harmful gases during construction projects, it became essential equipment for soldiers during World War I.

The Ironing Board

Sarah Boone, patented an improved design for the ironing board in 1982. Her design included a narrower and curved shape, making ironing sleeves and other curved garments easier.

The Folding Chair

John W. Hunter, patented the folding chair in 1944. His design included a lightweight and portable folding mechanism, making it popular for outdoor events, gatherings, and recreational activities.

The Home Security System

Marie Van Brittan Brown, patented the first home security system in 1966, featuring a closed-circuit television system, peepholes, and a two-way microphone, thereby providing homeowners with added security and peace of mind.

The Fire Escape

Joseph Winters patented an early design for the fire escape ladder in 1878. His invention provided a safe means of escaping from buildings during emergencies, saving countless lives.

Trailblazing Figures

Several of the most recent trailblazing figures are mentioned here: Oprah Winfrey—a global media leader, actress, and philanthropist, Letitia James—the first Black American and first woman to be elected Attorney General of New York, Fani Willis—the first woman to hold the position of District Attorney in Fulton County, Georgia, and Alvin J. Bragg, Jr.—the first Black American to be elected as Manhattan District Attorney in New York. There are many more examples; however, all the names mentioned are important because they should reflect the essence of the American Dream by overcoming obstacles, breaking barriers, and achieving success through hard work and resilience. These individuals should inspire the Black community to pursue dreams, regardless of the challenges one may face. It would help if people were inspired and understood the impact of representation and the importance of fighting and setting the stage for long-term systemic changes.

These inventors and trailblazing figures highlight the significant contributions of Black Americans. These examples demonstrate that Black individuals should cast away their intimidation and belief that White individuals are the dominant racial group—an idea rooted in an old belief system that can and must be broken. Individuals must embrace their worth, asserting equality to help challenge self-doubt, oppression, and discriminatory systems.

Moreover, it is anticipated and imperative that Black Americans, who are capable of obtaining, maintaining, and sustaining gainful employment within every job market, are encouraged to continue increasing their participation in a wide range of employment opportunities across various industries, such as doctors, plumbers, lawn care professionals, self-employments, engineers, small businesses, lawyers, electoral representatives, and many more. This increased participation is not only anticipated but also imperative due to several key factors. The U.S. is currently experiencing a significant demographic shift, with notable growth observed within Black communities. As a result, it is essential to have a workforce that adequately represents and serves the entire population. Greater representation in various industries ensures that the workforce reflects the diversity of the community, particularly in sectors like healthcare where cultural competence and understanding of different backgrounds can lead to better patient outcomes, as well as enhance the overall life expectancy, improve quality of life, and services provided across the U.S.

Additionally, to meet the needs of an increasingly diverse population, individuals are encouraged to work toward dismantling their old belief systems and create new ones by empowering themselves and pursuing their goals and aspirations. By advocating for their rights and believing in their abilities, individuals can achieve personal growth and success. It is important to stand up for dignity, support one another, and foster kindness within the community to inspire collective action and solidarity. This collective empowerment can lead to meaningful change and challenge old belief systems.

Chapter 6
Unraveling Tensions – Jewish Americans

In exploring the many aspects of human struggle, it is essential to look deeper into the unique experiences of different cultural and ethnic groups. Among these, the Jewish American community has faced various challenges historically and in contemporary society. From the shadows of persecution to the strains of assimilation, Jewish Americans face an environment influenced by various circumstances that influence their mental health. Throughout history, Jews have faced harsh persecution, including the horrors of the Holocaust (U.S. Holocaust Memorial Museum, n.d.-a, n.d.-b), which have left permanent scars on their collective psyche. Moreover, in contemporary society, Jewish Americans grapple with the ongoing threat of anti-Semitism, subtle and overt, alongside the complexities of identity formation and intergenerational transmission of trauma. These problems and the twin constraints of protecting cultural history while assimilating into mainstream culture create a complex list of experiences that require careful analysis and empathetic understanding.

Historical Trauma

The Jewish American experience is deeply intertwined with a history marked by persecution, discrimination, and genocide. From the horrors of the Holocaust to centuries of anti-Semitic sentiment, the collective trauma of the Jewish people weighs heavily on the psyche of many Jewish Americans. This intergenerational transmission of trauma can manifest in various forms, contributing to feelings of anxiety, depression, and unresolved grief. The indelible scars left by historical traumas echo through generations, shaping not only individual psyches but also family dynamics and communal ones. This enduring legacy of persecution fosters a heightened sense of vulnerability and hypervigilance as Jewish Americans get a hold of the complexities of identity, belonging, and cultural preservation in a world still plagued by bigotry and intolerance. Through acknowledgment, validation, and targeted interventions, society can begin to address the deep-seated wounds of the past and foster healing within the Jewish American community.

Identity Struggles

Balancing a sense of Jewish identity with the demands of American society can be a source of profound inner conflict. Jewish Americans may grapple with questions of assimilation versus cultural preservation, often feeling torn between embracing their heritage and fitting into mainstream culture. This struggle for identity can augment feelings of alienation and contribute to a sense of existential angst. The tension between maintaining a connection to one's roots and assimilating into broader society is a perennial challenge faced by many Jewish Americans, reflecting the complexities of dual identities in a multicultural world. This internal conflict is further compounded by external pressures to conform to societal norms and expectations, leading to a profound sense of dissonance and fragmentation within the individual psyche. Ultimately, reconciling these conflicting forces requires a nuanced understanding of identity formation, and self-acceptance, as well as the cultivation of supportive communities that honor and celebrate the richness of Jewish heritage while embracing the diversity of American life.

Anti-Semitism

Public outrage occurred because of the recent conflict between Israel and Palestine. People began to protest on the streets and show their solidarity with Palestinians in various impactful ways. National demonstrations broke out on November 4th, 2023, and January 13th, 2024, across the U.S., with crowds reaching hundreds and thousands (Bowman & Wamsley, 2023; Kirka et al., 2024). Messages about the conflict and visual aftermath of the bombings have spread across the Internet and social media. Reactions of horror, disbelief, and anger toward Israel have emerged, portraying Israelis and Jews as the face of genocide overnight.

Hostility toward Jews, in general, has increased all over the world. The growing anti-Semitism toward Jews is illustrated by the recent incline of online hate, the growing number of protests against the Israeli government, the vandalization of Jewish gravesites, and death threats directed toward synagogues. Events, such as the killings of 11 people at the synagogue in Pittsburgh, clearly display the harmful threats and prejudice against Jews (Hodge & Boddie, 2021). The current controversy surrounding the Israel–Palestine conflict is just the tip of the iceberg of the anti-Semitic sentiments growing in the U.S. alone. Religious hate crimes toward Jews have increased substantially in recent years, causing fear and unsettlement within Jewish communities.

It becomes increasingly apparent that the Jews are more targeted by hate crimes than any other (religious or not) minority group in society. The number of hate crimes committed against Jews has grown, but it should be noted that not all hate crimes have been reported. According to the National Crime Victimization Survey, people report only 46% of crimes to authorities (Hodge & Boddie, 2021), indicating that anti-Semitic crimes could be more prevalent than are made public. Even reported crimes can be impacted by reporting differences at various law enforcement agencies, leaving ample room for misinterpretation. However, based on what data are available, it can be safely assumed that Jewish Americans have been disproportionately targeted for hate crimes more than any other minority group in the country.

Not all instances of anti-Semitism are considered criminal acts, but they have the potential to spread hate, misinformation, and prejudice. Although not punishable by law enforcement, these acts of hate can still impact the well-being of Jewish individuals. Many Jewish Americans view anti-Semitism within the country as a significant issue, with some even considering it a severe problem. The number of antisemitic incidents has been on the rise in recent years. In the wake of the ongoing Palestine–Israel conflict, it is likely to further exacerbate anti-Jew sentiment in the country.

Intergenerational Conflict

Within Jewish American families, generational differences in attitudes and values can give rise to tensions and misunderstandings. Younger generations may struggle to uphold familial traditions while forging their paths in an ever-evolving world. Conflicting expectations and communication breakdowns can contribute to frustration, guilt, and disconnection from one's roots. This intergenerational friction reflects the broader societal shift toward individualism and cultural pluralism, challenging traditional notions of family cohesion and collective identity. The struggle to balance respect for cultural heritage with the desire for autonomy and self-expression can strain familial bonds, leading to conflicts over religious observance, cultural practices, and lifestyle choices.

Moreover, the rapid pace of social change and globalization further complicates this dynamic. Younger generations are exposed to diverse perspectives and values that may diverge from those of their parents and grandparents. These complex dynamics require open communication, mutual respect, and a willingness to embrace change while honoring the rich culture of Jewish tradition and heritage.

Dual Marginalization

Intersectionality adds another layer of complexity to the mental health struggles of Jewish Americans who belong to other marginalized groups, such as LGBTQ+ individuals, people of color, or those with disabilities. Multiple layers of identity can compound feelings of isolation and marginalization, exacerbating mental health challenges and amplifying the need for culturally competent care. For individuals at the intersection of these identities, experiences of discrimination and marginalization may be compounded, leading to heightened vulnerability to mental health issues such as anxiety, depression, and trauma.

Moreover, systemic barriers to accessing culturally responsive mental health services exacerbate disparities in care, leaving many Jewish Americans from marginalized backgrounds underserved and overlooked. Recognizing the diverse experiences and needs within the Jewish American community is essential for promoting holistic well-being and fostering inclusive spaces where all individuals can access the support and resources they need to thrive. This requires committing to intersectional advocacy, providing culturally competent care practices, and dismantling barriers to mental health equity for marginalized populations within the Jewish community and beyond.

Healing & Recovery

Despite the weight of these struggles, Jewish Americans have demonstrated remarkable strength. Drawing upon cultural traditions of faith, community support, and the determination of their ancestors, many find strength in solidarity and collective memory. Healing journeys may involve reclaiming cultural heritage, promoting activism against discrimination, and seeking culturally sensitive therapy to address mental health needs. Individuals who embrace the depth of Jewish tradition and history can rely on a heritage of tenacity and endurance to help them handle modern problems.

Moreover, the sense of belonging and connection within the Jewish community serves as a vital source of support and validation for those grappling with mental health issues. Through acts of solidarity, advocacy, and mutual aid, Jewish Americans can work together to create spaces of healing and empowerment where all individuals can thrive and flourish, regardless of their struggles or setbacks. This collective power serves as a beacon of hope, inspiring others to find strength in their journeys of healing and transformation.

Cultivating Empathy & Understanding

It is essential to foster greater empathy and understanding within both the Jewish community and society at large to address the unique mental health needs of Jewish Americans. These needs involve challenging stereotypes, amplifying marginalized voices, and creating inclusive spaces where individuals can feel seen, heard, and supported in their struggles. Breaking down barriers to mental health care requires confronting stigma and discrimination, dismantling misconceptions, and promoting culturally competent approaches that honor the diverse experiences and identities within the Jewish American community.

By centering the voices and perspectives of those most affected by mental health disparities, society can cultivate a more compassionate and inclusive understanding of mental illness, cultivating empathy, solidarity, and collective action to address systemic inequities. Building bridges of understanding and empathy across diverse communities strengthens people's collective capacity to support one another in need, creating a more resilient and compassionate society for all.

Disbelief & Heartbreak

Disbelief and heartbreak encapsulate the profound emotional turmoil experienced by many Jewish Americans as they confront the enduring specter of anti-Semitism and the atrocities of the past. Despite strides toward greater societal acceptance and progress, the persistence of anti-Semitic sentiment can evoke feelings of incredulity and despair. For many, it is a heart-wrenching realization that despite efforts to move forward, the shadows of history continue to cast a pall over their lives.

The disbelief stems from the sheer absurdity of prejudice and discrimination in a modern, supposedly enlightened society. It is a visceral reaction to the enduring presence of hate, manifested in subtle and overt acts. From casual slurs to violent attacks, each instance serves as a painful reminder of the fragility of progress and the pervasiveness of bigotry.

On the other hand, heartbreak emerges from the collective trauma ingrained in the Jewish American consciousness. This sorrow seeps into the soul upon hearing tales of persecution, the anguish of remembering loved ones lost to genocide, and the weight of inherited grief carried through generations. This sadness is a collective wound—a monument to a people's endurance and grief after enduring unspeakable pain. Disbelief and sorrow demand tremendous bravery and resilience. It entails addressing harsh facts, battling complacency, and forming relationships of solidarity with others who face similar challenges. Through communal grieving and remembrance, Jewish Americans find consolation in the community and gain strength from their predecessors' perseverance.

Moreover, transforming disbelief and heartbreak into action is a testament to the indomitable spirit of the Jewish American community. It channels grief into advocacy, leveraging pain as a catalyst for change and refusing to be silenced in the face of injustice. The following section contains information about stereotypes and fears faced by Jewish Americans to better understand their resilience.

Stereotypes & Fears

The stereotypes and fears surrounding Jewish Americans are profoundly unsettling and troubling, rooted in centuries-old prejudices that persist in U.S.

society. From the harmful portrayal of Jewish people as excessively wealthy and materialistic to insidious stereotypes about intelligence, business acumen, and even parenting styles, these misconceptions fuel mistrust and division. Moreover, the pervasive threat of anti-Semitism, whether overt or covert, instills a constant sense of apprehension and vigilance within the Jewish American community. Urgent action is required to dismantle these harmful stereotypes and address the underlying fears through rigorous education, empathetic dialogue, and absolute advocacy. Only then can we strive toward creating a society where Jewish Americans and all individuals feel genuinely valued, respected, and safe from discrimination and hatred.

Senseless Stereotypes

Wealthy & Materialistic

Jewish Americans are often portrayed as affluent and worldly, with a focus on financial success and status symbols. This stereotype may stem from historical occupations in finance and commerce and successful individuals in industries like entertainment and media. However, it overlooks the socioeconomic diversity within the Jewish community and ignores the historical discrimination and economic challenges many Jewish Americans have faced.

Greedy & Stingy

The stereotype of Jewish Americans as greedy or stingy perpetuates harmful misconceptions about their relationship with money. Although financial literacy and responsible budgeting may be valued in many Jewish households, this stereotype unfairly caricatures Jewish people as overly focused on personal gain at the expense of others. It fails to acknowledge the philanthropic contributions and communal values integral to Jewish traditions and culture.

Intellectual & Academic

Jewish Americans are often depicted as highly intelligent and academically successful, emphasizing education and intellectual pursuits. This stereotype may have roots in cultural values prioritizing learning and critical thinking as well as historical barriers to social mobility that encouraged academic achievement. However, it can also contribute to harmful stereotypes about other racial and ethnic groups, overlooking the diversity of interests and talents within the Jewish American population.

Business Savvy

Stereotypes of Jewish Americans as intelligent and successful in business may reflect historical roles in commerce and entrepreneurship. This stereotype can perpetuate harmful stereotypes about Jewish people and money, reinforcing misconceptions about greed or dishonesty. It also overlooks the diversity of careers and occupations within the Jewish American community, as well as the systemic barriers that have historically limited economic opportunities for marginalized groups.

Pushy or Aggressive

Stereotypes of Jewish Americans as assertive or aggressive may stem from cultural values that prioritize assertiveness and self-advocacy, as well as historical experiences of discrimination and persecution. However, this stereotype can perpetuate harmful stereotypes about Jewish people as overly aggressive or confrontational, contributing to prejudice and discrimination. It is essential to recognize that assertiveness is not inherently negative and can be valuable when advocating for oneself or others.

Culturally Insular

The stereotype of Jewish Americans as culturally insular may stem from historical experiences of persecution and discrimination, which have led to developing tight-knit communities and cultural preservation efforts. However, this stereotype overlooks the diversity of cultural experiences and identities within the Jewish American population, as well as the contributions of Jewish Americans to broader society. It can also perpetuate harmful stereotypes about exclusivity or elitism within Jewish communities, undermining efforts to foster inclusivity and diversity. While cultural insularity can help maintain a community's identity, fostering inclusivity and diversity, there should be potential for cultural exchange that requires a balance of preserving cultural heritage while actively engaging with the society at large that should benefit both the insular community and the larger society by creating a more inclusive and understanding environment through education awareness, and community engagement.

Overbearing or Overprotective Parents

Stereotypes of Jewish parents as overbearing or overprotective may reflect cultural values that prioritize family and education, as well as historical experiences of persecution that have fostered a strong sense of communal solidarity. However, this stereotype can perpetuate harmful stereotypes about Jewish families and parenting styles, contributing to prejudice and discrimination. It is essential to recognize that parenting styles vary widely within the Jewish American community, and generalizations can be harmful and misleading.

Ethnically Homogeneous

The stereotype of Jewish Americans as ethnically homogeneous overlooks the diversity of cultural backgrounds, religious practices, and ethnic identities within the Jewish community. Jewish Americans come from a wide range of backgrounds, including Ashkenazi, Sephardic, Mizrahi, and other Jewish ethnic groups, each with its own traditions, languages, and customs. This stereotype can perpetuate harmful misconceptions about Jewish identity and contribute to erasure and marginalization within and outside the Jewish community.

Politically Liberal

Stereotypes of Jewish Americans as politically liberal may reflect historical alliances with progressive causes, social justice movements, and shared values of equality and justice. However, this stereotype overlooks the diversity of political opinions within the Jewish American population, which includes individuals with a wide range of political affiliations and ideologies. It is essential to recognize that Jewish Americans, like any other group, hold various political views and engage in political activism across various issues and concerns.

Comedy & Entertainment

Stereotypes of Jewish Americans as disproportionately represented in comedy and entertainment industries may reflect historical contributions from Jewish comedians, writers, actors, and filmmakers. This issue can perpetuate harmful stereotypes about Jewish people as naturally humorous, overlooking the diversity of talents and interests within the Jewish American population. It is essential to recognize that Jewish Americans, like any other group, are individuals with varied interests and talents, offering contributions to society beyond entertainment.

Lingering Fears

Anti-Semitic Violence & Hate Crimes

Jewish Americans fear physical harm or attacks motivated by anti-Semitic hatred. This fear is grounded in the sobering reality of historical and contemporary instances of violence targeting Jewish individuals and communities. The memory of tragic events, such as synagogue shootings and acts of vandalism against Jewish institutions, looms large, creating a pervasive sense of vulnerability and insecurity.

Discrimination in Employment, Housing, or Education

Jewish Americans fear facing discrimination or bias in various aspects of life, including employment opportunities, housing availability, and educational opportunities. This fear is rooted in experiences of systemic prejudice and exclusion, where individuals may be unfairly judged or overlooked due to their Jewish identity. The specter of discrimination can undermine confidence and limit opportunities for advancement, leading to frustration and disillusionment.

Social Exclusion or Ostracism

Jewish Americans fear being marginalized or ostracized within their communities or social circles due to their religious beliefs or cultural practices. This fear arises from the threat of social stigma or discrimination, where individuals may face judgment or alienation for expressing their Jewish identity openly. The fear of rejection can lead to self-censorship and reluctance to fully engage with one's cultural heritage, resulting in isolation and disconnection from one's community.

Holocaust Denial or Minimization

Jewish Americans fear the erasure or distortion of Holocaust history, including denial or minimization of the atrocities committed against Jewish people during World War II. This fear is grounded in the need to preserve the memory of the Holocaust as a warning against future acts of genocide and as a tribute to the millions of lives lost. The denial of historical truth not only dishonors the memory of survivors and victims but also perpetuates dangerous ideologies rooted in hatred and intolerance.

Being Targeted or Scapegoated During Times of Political or Social Unrest

Jewish Americans fear being scapegoated or targeted during periods of political upheaval or social unrest. This fear is fueled by historical precedents of anti-Semitic rhetoric and violence during times of crisis. Jewish communities have been unfairly blamed for societal problems or used as convenient scapegoats by political leaders seeking to deflect attention from their failures.

Prejudice or Harassment Based on Stereotypes About Jewish People

Jewish Americans fear encountering prejudice or harassment based on harmful stereotypes about Jewish people, such as accusations of being overly wealthy, manipulative, or controlling. This fear is rooted in the pervasive influence of anti-Semitic tropes and stereotypes in shaping public perception.

These perceptions lead to misconceptions and biases that can manifest in interpersonal interactions and institutional practices.

Threats to Synagogue Security or Jewish Communal Spaces

Jewish Americans fear for the safety and security of their synagogues and other communal spaces, where they gather for worship, education, and community events. This fear is heightened by the increasing frequency of threats, vandalism, and violence targeting Jewish institutions, which serve as symbols of Jewish identity. The need to protect these spaces from harm underscores the urgency of addressing anti-Semitic extremism and ensuring the safety of all members of the Jewish community.

Online Harassment or Cyberbullying

Jewish Americans fear experiencing harassment or cyberbullying online due to their Jewish identity. This fear is fueled by the anonymity and accessibility of online platforms, where individuals may face hateful messages, threats, or trolling based on their religious beliefs or cultural background. The prevalence of online hate speech and misinformation targeting Jewish people underscores the need for robust measures to combat online extremism and protect vulnerable communities from digital threats.

Rising Extremism & Hate Groups

Jewish Americans fear the resurgence of extremism and hate groups promoting anti-Semitic ideologies. This fear is grounded in the alarming rise of hate crimes and extremist rhetoric targeting Jewish communities, fueled by conspiracy theories, White supremacist ideologies, and online radicalization. The proliferation of hate groups poses a significant threat to the safety and well-being of Jewish Americans, necessitating coordinated efforts to counter hate speech, monitor extremist activities, and address the root causes of radicalization.

Intergenerational Trauma

Jewish Americans fear the intergenerational transmission of trauma and its impact on mental health and well-being within the Jewish community. This fear is rooted in the collective memory of historical traumas, such as the Holocaust, pogroms, and persecution, which continue to reverberate through subsequent generations. The legacy of trauma can manifest in various forms, including anxiety, depression, and PTSD, affecting individuals and families across their lifespans. Addressing intergenerational trauma requires sensitivity, compassion, and access to culturally competent mental health services to support healing within the Jewish community.

Impact of Recent Events: Rising Anti-Semitism

Anti-Zionism is a political movement established back in the late 19th century in response to the growing anti-Semitism toward Jewish nationals. Since the birth of the country of Israel, the region has experienced several wars, with the most recent one occurring in 2023 (Segev, 2024). The movement grew in strength in response to the recent controversies surrounding the occupation and attacks on the state of Palestine, which attracted the attention of people all over the world. Palestine refused the occupation of Israel and adopted the Jewish identity, which raised a lot of racist, anticolonial sentiments toward the global Jewish population. Israel, backed by several powerful allies such as the U.S., built a system where Palestinians were considered stateless citizens without human rights, unlike the Jewish Israeli population, whom the government favored in terms of resources, protection, and citizenship. The popular media labeled the Israeli state as *terroristic, undemocratic, cruel,* and *anti-Semitic* in response to the growing support for Palestine. Many publicly claimed that the Israeli state needed to be held accountable for the ongoing violations of the human rights of Palestinians, which resulted in house demolitions, extrajudicial killings, and indefinite detention of the Palestinian people.

In the wake of these recent events, the specter of rising anti-Semitism looms ominously, casting a dark shadow over the collective psyche of Jewish Americans. The palpable fear and anxiety stemming from increased incidents of hate speech, vandalism, and violence targeting Jewish communities evoke a profound sense of vulnerability and despair. Each new report of anti-Semitic rhetoric or attacks serves as a painful reminder of the persistent threat posed by bigotry and intolerance. The relentless onslaught of hatred leaves many Jewish Americans grappling with overwhelming feelings of fear, anger, and helplessness as they deal with a world where their safety and security are constantly under siege.

The mental toll of rising anti-Semitism extends far beyond the immediate impact of individual incidents, permeating every aspect of daily life and exacerbating existing mental health struggles. The constant vigilance required to safeguard against potential threats fosters a pervasive sense of hypervigilance and paranoia, eroding feelings of safety and trust in one's surroundings. Moreover, the insidious nature of anti-Semitic rhetoric in mainstream media and online platforms amplifies feelings of isolation and alienation, fueling a sense of existential dread and despair.

The psychological trauma inflicted by rising anti-Semitism reverberates through the Jewish American community, leaving deep scars on the collective psyche. Many individuals grapple with symptoms of PTSD, depression, and anxiety as they struggle to process the trauma of living in a world where hatred and prejudice thrive. Sleep disturbances, flashbacks, and intrusive thoughts plague survivors of anti-Semitic violence, while others wrestle with feelings of guilt, shame, and survivor's guilt in the face of ongoing persecution.

The impact of rising anti-Semitism on mental health underscores the urgent need for comprehensive support and intervention to address the psychological fallout of hate and bigotry. Culturally sensitive mental health services, trauma-informed care, and community-based support networks play a crucial role in helping Jewish Americans cope with the profound psychological toll of anti-Semitic persecution. By prioritizing mental health awareness, advocacy, and access to resources, we can begin to heal the wounds inflicted by hatred and build a more resilient and compassionate society for all.

Coping With Collective Anguish & Frustration

Amidst the tumult of collective anguish and frustration, Jewish Americans find themselves grappling with a profound sense of despair and disillusionment. The weight of historical traumas, compounded by the resurgence of anti-Semitism and societal injustices, bears down heavily on the shoulders of the community. Individuals deal with an environment riddled with uncertainty and instability, relying on coping mechanisms stretched to their limits, attempting to find consolation in the turmoil. In the face of unending suffering, many Jewish Americans retreat inward, finding solace in social relationships and cultural traditions. Nevertheless, even within the embrace of community, the echoes of anguish reverberate, each shared burden serving as a poignant reminder of the collective struggle. Coping with the weight of generational trauma, survivors' guilt, and existential dread, individuals confront the stark reality of living in a world rife with prejudice and hatred.

The constant onslaught of injustice and prejudice generates a tide of boiling hatred and frustration, threatening to consume the spirit in a hurricane of emotion. Individuals grapple to find purpose amidst insurmountable challenges as their optimism and fortitude diminish.

The collective trauma of witnessing systemic oppression and societal indifference leaves scars that run deep, casting a long shadow over the soul. Jewish Americans tap into a wellspring of strength and determination inherited over generations. Nevertheless, even the most resilient face trials during tragedy, confronting existential questions amid chaos. Coping with the collective anguish and frustration demands courage, compassion, and a steadfast commitment to bring healing and solidarity within the community.

In the face of seemingly insurmountable challenges, Jewish Americans persevere, drawing strength from the bonds of shared experience and the determination of their ancestors. Coping with the collective anguish and frustration is a journey fraught with hardship and uncertainty. Nevertheless, it is also a testament to the indomitable human spirit and the enduring power of hope. Through solidarity, advocacy, and mutual support, individuals confront the darkness with resolve, striving to build a brighter future for themselves and generations yet to come. To aid in this journey, some ways to improve quality of life are discussed in the next section.

Ways to Improve Long-Term Quality of Life

Jewish Americans face complex barriers and possibilities in their quest for a higher quality of life. Confronted by an unyielding tide of challenges, individuals actively seek sustainable solutions to foster long-term well-being and dedication within their community. Employing a multifaceted approach that embraces cultural empowerment, advocacy, and holistic care, Jewish Americans are dedicated to charting a course toward a brighter and more promising future.

Cultural Empowerment & Identity

Strengthening cultural identity and connection to heritage is a cornerstone for enhancing the quality of life in the long term. Individuals develop a feeling of belonging and tenacity during challenges by taking pride in their Jewish traditions, language, and history. Celebrating cultural diversity within the community fosters solidarity and unity, empowering individuals to confront systemic challenges with strength.

Community Building & Support Networks

Investing in community building and support networks provides vital resources and solidarity to deal with life's challenges. Establishing safe spaces for dialogue, mutual aid, and collective action fosters a sense of belonging and connection within the community. By implementing supportive relationships and networks, individuals access valuable emotional, social, and material support to enhance their quality of life and long-term well-being.

Advocacy & Social Justice

Advocating for social justice and equity is integral to improving the quality of life of Jewish Americans and other marginalized communities. Individuals work toward creating a more just and inclusive society by challenging systemic injustices, discrimination, and inequality. Engaging in advocacy efforts, grassroots organizing, and policy reform initiatives empowers individuals to address the root causes of social disparities and foster systemic changes that benefit the entire community.

Holistic Health & Wellness Practices

Prioritizing holistic health and wellness promotes long-term well-being. Mindfulness, stress management skills, and self-care rituals can help people cope with the psychological effects of tragedy and trauma. Accessing culturally competent mental health services, therapy, and support groups provides vital resources to address mental health challenges and foster healing within the community.

Education & Lifelong Learning

Investing in education and lifelong learning opportunities empowers individuals to pursue personal growth, professional development, and social mobility. Individuals enhance their adaptability in changing circumstances by prioritizing education and skill-building initiatives. Access to quality education, vocational training, and mentorship programs equips individuals with the tools and knowledge to thrive and succeed in diverse contexts.

Interfaith & Intercultural Dialogue

Interfaith and intercultural dialogue promotes understanding, empathy, and cooperation across diverse communities. Jewish Americans build bridges of solidarity and mutual respect by engaging in meaningful dialogue and collaboration with individuals from different backgrounds. Promoting interfaith partnerships, multicultural initiatives, and community engagement strengthens social cohesion and fosters a sense of interconnectedness within broader society.

Civic Engagement & Political Participation

Active civic engagement and political participation are essential for shaping policies and decisions that impact the quality of life for Jewish Americans and other marginalized communities. By exercising their rights to vote, advocate, and participate in democratic processes, individuals amplify their voices and influence positive change. Engaging in community organizing, voter mobilization, and advocacy campaigns empowers individuals to address systemic injustices and advocate for policies that promote equity and social justice.

By embracing these holistic approaches and collaborative efforts, Jewish

Americans work toward improving their quality of life and providing strength within the community. Through a commitment to cultural empowerment, social justice, and holistic well-being, society may pave the way for a brighter future grounded in solidarity, compassion, and collective action.

Chapter 7
Unraveling Tensions – Muslim Americans

According to Rosenberg (2024), Muslims in America today face a myriad of struggles that profoundly impact their mental well-being, leaving them grappling with a range of emotional and psychological challenges. These struggles are rooted in a climate of pervasive Islamophobia, discrimination, and social marginalization, which permeate various aspects of their daily lives. Particularly in the Western areas of the world, Muslims tend to be subject to prejudice, exclusion, discrimination, and violence. They are seen as foreigners and often perceived as not belonging to their country of residence, even if they were born there. In countries such as the U.S., Muslims experience racist and xenophobic sentiments that marginalize them in society (Wang et al., 2020). Nearly half of all Muslim Americans have experienced some form of discrimination or prejudice due to their religion.

One of the most alarming and distressing struggles that Muslims in America contend with is the relentless wave of Islamophobia that has swept the nation. From hate speech and discriminatory policies to violent hate crimes and acts of terrorism, Muslims face a constant barrage of bigotry and prejudice. The fear of being targeted solely based on their religious identity weighs heavily on their minds, fueling anxiety, hypervigilance, and a pervasive sense of insecurity.

The impact of Islamophobia extends beyond individual experiences of discrimination to systemic injustices that permeate various institutions and sectors of society. Muslims face employment discrimination, educational barriers, and profiling by law enforcement agencies, which not only limit their opportunities for advancement but also erode their sense of dignity and belonging. The pervasive nature of these structural inequalities contributes to feelings of powerlessness, frustration, and resentment, exacerbating mental health struggles and perpetuating cycles of marginalization.

The intersectionality of identity compounds the mental health challenges faced by Muslims in America, particularly for those who belong to other marginalized groups. LGBTQ+ Muslims, Black Muslims, and Muslim immigrants confront overlapping layers of discrimination, prejudice, and social exclusion, which intersect to create unique and complex experiences of marginalization. Steering through multiple forms of oppression can intensify feelings of alienation, internalized stigma, and identity conflict, leading to heightened levels of anxiety, depression, and psychological distress.

The psychological toll of these struggles is profound, with many Muslims in America experiencing elevated rates of mental health disorders compared to the general population. Studies have documented higher rates of depression, anxiety, PTSD, and suicidality among Muslim individuals, reflecting the cumulative impact of chronic stress, discrimination, and trauma on their mental well-being (Eskin et al., 2020; Tineo et al., 2021; Wang et al., 2020). The stigma surrounding mental health within the Muslim community, coupled with barriers to accessing culturally competent care, further exacerbates the challenges faced by those seeking support and treatment.

Additionally, Muslims in America often grapple with intergenerational tensions within their families and communities stemming from cultural clashes, religious conservatism, and generational divides. Conflicting expectations and values between different generations can create significant stress and strain familial relationships, leading to feelings of isolation, guilt, and emotional turmoil. The pressure to establish an understanding between traditional cultural norms and Western societal expectations can fuel identity crises and lead to a sense of disconnection from both worlds, further intensifying psychological distress.

Despite these enormous hurdles, Muslims in America display extraordinary diligence. Many draws on the strength of their faith, communities' support, and ancestors' dedication to understanding the complexities of their lived experiences. Advocacy efforts, community organizing, and grassroots initiatives aimed at combating Islamophobia and promoting social justice play a crucial role in empowering Muslims to assert their rights, challenge stereotypes, and demand systemic change.

The struggles faced by Muslims in America are multifaceted, deeply entrenched, and profoundly concerning. From the scourge of Islamophobia to the intersecting layers of discrimination and social marginalization, Muslims confront a host of mental health challenges that demand urgent attention and action. By addressing the root causes of these struggles, promoting awareness and empathy, and advocating for inclusive policies and practices, society can work toward creating a society where all individuals, regardless of their religious or cultural backgrounds, can live free from fear, stigma, and oppression.

Disbelief & Heartbreak

According to Rehman and Hanley (2023), there has been a significant increase in discrimination and racism toward Muslims ever since the 9/11 tragedy. Paired with the growing Western nationalism, the anti-Islamic rhetoric has fed negative stereotypes about Islam, as people share a growing fear and uncertainty toward Muslims. *Islamophobia* began to be used as a term in the late

20th century, described as a hostility toward Islam and Muslims, characterized by strong dislike or fear (Rehman & Hanley, 2023). Islamophobia has had various adverse effects on the lives of Muslims all over the world, with many suffering from mental health illnesses and psychological distress (Rehman & Hanley, 2023).

The relentless barrage of discrimination and prejudice takes a toll on the emotional well-being of Muslim Americans, leaving them shattered and emotionally depleted. The constant fear of being singled out or subjected to hate-fueled attacks engenders a pervasive sense of vulnerability and insecurity, undermining their sense of safety and belonging in their own country. The weight of this burden, compounded by the trauma of witnessing their community vilified and demonized, leaves many Muslim Americans grappling with feelings of hopelessness and despair.

In confronting the profound sense of disbelief and heartbreak that accompanies Islamophobia and discrimination, Muslim Americans are compelled to reckon with the stark realities of their existence and the urgent need for systemic change. They draw on the strength of their faith, the unity of their community, and the commitment to justice and equality to go through the turbulent waters of bigotry and hatred. Despite the immense challenges they face, Muslim Americans stand firm in their resolve to challenge prejudice, dismantle systemic barriers, and forge a path toward a more inclusive and equitable society for themselves and future generations.

Stereotypes & Fears

Global terrorism is perhaps the most prominent source of fear and stereotypes among Muslims worldwide. The rise of terrorist organizations such as ISIS and Al-Qaeda has significantly affected the perceptions of the public toward Muslims and further fueled the prejudices against them (Von Sikorski et al., 2020). Moreover, public media coverage of Muslims has been generally negative and linked to extremist or terrorist groups, causing many to develop a fear toward ordinary Muslims living in Western countries.

Little differentiation has been made between ordinary Muslims and members of extremist groups, which has led to the belief that all Muslims are similar. The out-group homogeneity effect means that many members of the public tend to assume that the outgroup members, such as individual Muslim terrorists, tend to represent the rest of the ingroup members, i.e., the entire Western Muslim population. Such stereotypes and coverage by the media have fueled harmful and inaccurate representations of Muslims all over the world, especially in Western countries where they are a minority.

Stereotypes

Terrorist

The portrayal of Muslim Americans as terrorists or sympathizers of extremist ideologies is not only pervasive but also deeply damaging. This harmful stereotype is rooted in a distorted narrative that conflates Islam with terrorism, perpetuating fear and discrimination against Muslim individuals and communities. Despite the overwhelming evidence to the contrary, which highlights the peaceful and diverse nature of Islam, this stereotype persists, casting suspicion and mistrust on innocent individuals solely based on their religious affiliation. This stereotype not only vilifies Muslims but also contributes to their social and economic marginalization, as they face heightened scrutiny and profiling in various aspects of their lives. From airport security screenings to employment opportunities, Muslims encounter barriers and biases that impede their ability to participate fully in society. This systemic discrimination infringes upon their civil liberties and undermines the fundamental principles of justice and equality upon which the U.S. was founded.

The perpetuation of the terrorist stereotype fosters a climate of fear and hostility toward Muslim communities, exacerbating feelings of alienation and insecurity. Muslim individuals often face hate crimes, verbal abuse, and harassment as they go through a society that views them with suspicion and apprehension. This constant threat of violence and discrimination takes a toll on their mental health and well-being, leading to heightened levels of anxiety, depression, and trauma.

Oppressed Women

The stereotype of Muslim women as oppressed and subservient is not only inaccurate but also profoundly harmful. It perpetuates a narrow and homogenized view of Muslim women, ignoring the rich diversity of their experiences, identities, and contributions to society. This stereotype erases the agency and autonomy of Muslim women, reducing them to passive victims of patriarchal oppression and religious conservatism. In reality, Muslim women defy simplistic categorizations and occupy a broad spectrum of roles and identities. Muslim women have significantly contributed to various fields, including science, literature, politics, and the arts, challenging stereotypes and breaking barriers in pursuing their aspirations and goals.

The following subsections contain examples of some Muslim women who have overcome stereotypes of oppression and made significant contributions in various fields worldwide:

Malala Yousafzai. Malala, is a Muslim and a Pakistani activist for female education and the youngest Nobel Prize laureate, has fearlessly stood up against persecution from the Taliban for advocating for girls' education. Despite facing adversity, she continues to be a global advocate for children's rights (Khan et al., 2021). She is considered one of the most renowned figures in Pakistani society, with numerous schools named in her honor as a testament to her strength and bravery in inspiring women to pursue further education (Khan et al., 2021).

Ilhan Omar. Ilhan Omar is a Somali American politician who became one of the first Muslim women elected to the U.S. Congress (Maha, 2019). Through her advocacy for social justice, immigration reform, and women's rights (Representative of Ilhan Omar, 2024), she has challenged the narrative of Muslim women being submissive and oppressed. She has courageously overcome the discrimination and Islamophobia that has disadvantaged many Muslim women in the Western world (Alkazemi et al., 2021).

Shirin Ebadi. Shirin Ebadi is an Iranian lawyer and human rights activist who was awarded the Nobel Peace Prize for promoting democracy and human rights, particularly the rights of women and children in Iran (The Editors of Encyclopaedia Britannica, 2024). Despite facing pressure to comply with oppressive misinterpretations of Islam that marginalized women in Iranian society, Ebadi stood firm in her advocacy, facing punishments, threats, and sanctions with unwavering resolve (Dalfino & Allamneni, 2022).

Tawakkol Karman. Tawakkol Karman is a Yemeni journalist, politician, and human rights activist who became the first Arab woman to win the Nobel Peace Prize for her role in the Arab Spring protests in Yemen (The Nobel Prize, n.d.). In addition to her remarkable achievements, she established a foundation in Istanbul to aid further development in the country. Karman openly criticized Saudi Arabia and the United Arab Emirates for their roles in the Yemen war, showcasing her staunch dedication to justice and peace (Mermier, 2023).

Rashida Tlaib. Rashida Tlaib is a Palestinian-American politician who became one of the first Muslim women elected to the U.S. Congress (Maha, 2019). She is known for her advocacy of progressive policies and social justice issues, Tlaib was the first woman (representing Michigan) and Palestinian American woman to be elected to U.S. Congress (Maha, 2019).

Faatimah Knight. Faatimah Knight is an American Muslim activist who founded the #Muslims4Abolition movement. Knight advocated for criminal justice reform and racial equity within Muslim communities.

Yusra Mardini. Yusra Mardini is a Syrian refugee and Olympic swimmer who competed in the 2016 Summer Olympics in Rio de Janeiro. Her bravery in rescuing fellow refugees by swimming across the Aegean Sea, showcased her courage and selflessness (Kulkarni, 2024). She has been portrayed as a hero for her actions, which somewhat downplayed her performance at the Olympics. Mardini's humanitarian efforts have solidified her as a global inspiration and role model (Michelini, 2021).

Ibtihaj Muhammad. Ibtihaj Muhammad, an American saber fencer, made history as the first Muslim American woman to wear a hijab while competing for the U.S. in the Olympics. She advocated for Muslim representation in sports and society, breaking down stereotypes of Muslim women in sports and removing cultural and religious mores (Grubic, 2022). This act may serve as a legacy for female Olympians for decades to come (Magrath, 2022).

Nadiya Hussain. Nadiya Hussain is a British-Bangladeshi chef, author, and television presenter who gained fame after winning the sixth series of *The Great British Bake Off* in 2015 (Lagerwey, 2018). She leveraged her platform as the first Muslim woman to win the competition to challenge stereotypes and promote diversity in the culinary world, overcoming widespread criticism, backbiting, and even hatred, thereby serving as an inspiration for women of color in British society (Lagerwey, 2018).

Amal Clooney. Amal Clooney is married to actor George Clooney as of 2014, and she is an international human rights lawyer, activist, and author, renowned for her representation of clients in high-profile cases involving international law and human rights violations, which includes defending the rights of individuals who are Muslims. She advocates for refugees, women's rights, and freedom of speech (Stern Milch, 2023). Notably, her impactful address at a UN meeting shed light on the devastating repercussions of the genocide in Iraq, as she tirelessly fought for justice on behalf of the victims of abduction and rape by ISIS members (Kehl, 2021).

Fanatical Beliefs

The pervasive stereotype that Muslim Americans hold fanatical or extremist beliefs is not only misleading but also harmful. This oversimplification fails to acknowledge the rich diversity of religious beliefs and practices within the Muslim community, reducing a complex and multifaceted faith tradition to a monolithic entity defined by extremism. By perpetuating this stereotype, individuals and society at large reinforce negative perceptions of Islam as inherently radical or violent, further stigmatizing Muslim Americans and contributing to their marginalization and discrimination. However, the Muslim community encompasses a broad spectrum of religious beliefs, interpretations, and practices, reflecting the diverse cultural, ethnic, and theological backgrounds of its members. Although some individuals may adhere to Islam's conservative interpretations, most Muslim Americans espouse moderate or progressive views by emphasizing values of peace, compassion, and social justice. These individuals reject violence and extremism in all forms while actively working to promote harmony and understanding within their communities and the U.S. society at large.

Foreignness & Otherness

The pervasive stereotype of perceiving Muslim Americans as foreign or "other" is not only inaccurate but also deeply damaging. Despite many Muslim Americans being born and raised in the U.S., they often face this harmful stereotype. This stereotype reinforces feelings of alienation and marginalization within their own country. The notion that Muslim Americans do not belong in American society perpetuates division and exclusion, undermining the principles of inclusivity and diversity that are fundamental to the American identity.

This stereotype often overlooks the diverse experiences and backgrounds within the Muslim community, which encompasses individuals from various ethnicities, cultures, and nationalities. Many Muslim Americans have diverse and multifaceted identities that intersect with other marginalized communities, further complicating their sense of belonging in American society. By reducing them to a homogeneous group defined by their religious affiliation, this stereotype erases their individuality and perpetuates harmful misconceptions.

Lack of Integration

The stereotype of Muslim Americans as unwilling or unable to integrate into American society is not only unfounded but also harmful. It perpetuates a false narrative that Muslim Americans are somehow inherently isolationist and resistant to assimilation in their communities, undermining their contributions to various aspects of American life and hindering efforts toward social cohesion and inclusion. Moreover, the stereotype of Muslim Americans as insular and resistant to assimilation overlooks the diverse experiences and backgrounds of the individuals within the Muslim community. Many actively engage in civic and community activities, volunteer work, and interfaith dialogue, forging connections and building bridges across diverse communities. They embrace American values of freedom, equality, and opportunity while celebrating their cultural heritage and religious identity.

Fears

Discrimination & Islamophobia

With the never-ending fear of discrimination and Islamophobia across multiple domains, including employment, education, housing, and public spaces, the West seems like it is not really about living freely. This pervasive climate of suspicion cultivates heightened levels of anxiety and distress as individuals realize the daily challenges of bigotry and prejudice. The looming threat of marginalization and targeting due to their religious identity exacerbates feelings of vulnerability and insecurity within the Muslim community. Such fears hinder their ability to fully engage in society and erode their sense of belonging and acceptance. Consequently, Muslims in America grapple with the daunting reality of a society rife with systemic biases and prejudices against them.

Hate Crimes & Violence

As hate crimes targeting Muslims continue to rise, many in the Muslim American community live in fear of becoming victims of violence or harassment solely due to their religious identity. Instances of vandalism, physical assaults, and verbal abuse further worsen the pervasive sense of insecurity and vulnerability felt by Muslims across the nation. These acts not only threaten their physical safety but also inflict lasting psychological harm, deepening the divide and eroding the sense of safety and belonging within the Muslim community. Such fear casts a long shadow over daily life, prompting individuals to become cautious of their surroundings.

Surveillance & Profiling

Often living in fear of surveillance and proofing, Muslims in America harbor apprehensions about being subjected to surveillance, profiling, and monitoring by law enforcement solely because of their religious or ethnic identity. The erosion of civil liberties and privacy rights intensifies feelings of distrust and alienation within the community as individuals confront the looming threat of unjust targeting or surveillance. This persistent fear of unwarranted scrutiny undermines their sense of security and diminishes trust in institutions meant to protect them. Consequently, Muslims in America live their daily lives under a cloud of suspicion and uncertainty, perpetuating a cycle of distrust and alienation from broader society.

Social Exclusion & Marginalization

Muslims in America have concerns about social exclusion or

marginalization within their communities and broader society due to prevalent stereotypes, misconceptions, and negative perceptions surrounding Islam and Muslims. The pressure to reconcile mainstream cultural norms with the preservation of religious and cultural identities can induce feelings of isolation and disconnection in Muslims residing in the U.S. This fear of being ostracized or misunderstood perpetuates a sense of alienation and hinders meaningful social integration, complicating efforts to foster mutual understanding and cohesion across diverse communities. As a result, Muslims in America grapple with the delicate balance of maintaining their identity while striving for acceptance and belonging in a society fraught with prejudice and misunderstanding.

Political Backlash & Policy Changes

Muslims in America harbor apprehensions about political backlash and policy changes explicitly targeting their community, such as travel bans, surveillance programs, and immigration restrictions. These discriminatory policies not only infringe on their rights and freedoms but also sow seeds of uncertainty and insecurity regarding their place in American society. The specter of exclusion and marginalization looms large as they grapple with the implications of such measures, which undermine their sense of belonging, exacerbate divisions, and erode the principles of justice and equality upon which the nation was founded. As a result, Muslims in America confront a daunting reality, with challenges to their rights and dignity as equal members of society.

The Rising Islamophobia

In recent years, the specter of Islamophobia has cast a dark shadow over the Muslim American community, permeating various aspects of daily life and exacerbating existing tensions within society. This surge in Islamophobia, fueled by political rhetoric, media sensationalism, and deep-seated prejudices, has had far-reaching implications for Muslims in America, reshaping their experiences, perceptions, and sense of security. At the heart of the rising Islamophobia phenomenon, lies a complex interplay of social, political, and cultural factors that have contributed to the demonization and vilification of Islam and Muslims. The aftermath of tragic events, such as the 9/11 attacks and subsequent acts of terrorism perpetrated by individuals claiming allegiance to extremist ideologies, has fueled a climate of fear and suspicion toward Muslims, casting them as perpetual suspects in the eyes of many.

One of the most profound impacts of rising Islamophobia is the erosion of trust and social cohesion within American society. Muslims in America increasingly find themselves marginalized, stigmatized, and ostracized as pervasive stereotypes and misconceptions perpetuate negative perceptions of their faith and identity. The prevalence of anti-Muslim sentiment in public discourse, coupled with discriminatory policies and practices, has created a hostile environment where Muslims are viewed with suspicion and subjected to systemic injustices.

The rise in Islamophobia has also manifested in alarming rates of hate crimes and discrimination targeting Muslims across the nation. Acts of vandalism against mosques, verbal abuse, physical assaults, and even deadly attacks have become disturbingly common occurrences, instilling fear and insecurity within the Muslim community. The normalization of anti-Muslim rhetoric and hate speech in political discourse and media coverage has emboldened perpetrators of Islamophobic violence, amplifying feelings of vulnerability and alienation among Muslims in America.

If we talk about the impact of rising Islamophobia, let us just say it extends beyond individual acts of violence and discrimination to broader systemic inequalities and injustices faced by Muslims in various spheres of life. The pervasive nature of Islamophobia permeates institutional structures, perpetuating disparities and hindering opportunities for social and economic advancement within the Muslim community. The issue is not merely limited to economic advancement; the sheer lunacy against Muslims in America has also taken a psychological toll on the community, and this absurdity cannot be shoved under the rug anymore. Muslim Americans grapple with feelings of anxiety, fear, and uncertainty as they spend their lives in a society that views them through a lens of suspicion and mistrust. The constant vigilance required to protect themselves and their families from potential harm, takes a toll on their mental well-being, leading to heightened levels of stress, trauma, and psychological distress.

In addition to its immediate impacts, rising Islamophobia has long-term consequences for the social fabric and democratic principles of American society. Under the guise of national security and counterterrorism efforts, erasing civil liberties and constitutional rights undermines the foundational values of freedom, equality, and justice. Muslims in America face intrusive surveillance, profiling, and harassment by law enforcement agencies, further eroding trust in public institutions and perpetuating feelings of alienation and disenfranchisement.

Addressing the impact of rising Islamophobia requires a multifaceted approach that addresses the root causes of prejudice and discrimination while promoting understanding, empathy, and inclusion within society. Education plays a crucial role in challenging stereotypes and misconceptions about Islam and Muslims, giving rise to interfaith dialogue and cultural competency among diverse communities. Political leaders and policymakers must also take proactive measures to combat Islamophobia by enacting policies that protect the rights and dignity of all individuals, regardless of their religious or cultural background.

Moreover, media outlets and public figures have a responsibility to refrain from sensationalizing and perpetuating negative stereotypes about Islam and Muslims. Instead, the media should focus on promoting accurate and nuanced representations that reflect the diversity and complexity of the Muslim American experience. Furthermore, community-based initiatives and grassroots organizations play a vital role in empowering Muslims to advocate for their rights, build solidarity with other marginalized communities, and challenge the structures of oppression and injustice that perpetuate Islamophobia.

Community Unity: Strategies for Overcoming Collective Challenges

Regarding societal injustices and enduring obstacles, Muslim Americans have confronted tumultuous waters, contending with a collective sense of anguish and frustration. The burden of discrimination, prejudice, and systemic inequities exacts a profound toll on the mental and emotional fortitude of community members. Persistent biases and structural barriers compound individuals' challenges, giving a pervasive atmosphere of unease and discontent. Daily life becomes a daunting task as the collective struggle against societal injustices weighs heavily on the hearts and minds of Muslim Americans, shaping their experiences and perceptions in profound ways. Therefore, this section discusses some strategies employed by Muslim Americans to cope with these daunting realities:

Resilient Communities

Based on their communities' fortitude, Muslim Americans derive comfort from the solidarity fostered through shared trials and mutual assistance. Community hubs, such as mosques, community centers, and grassroots organizations, emerge as sanctuaries where individuals can find solace, direction, and unity. Within these safe havens, members lean on one another for support, exchange guidance, and solidify bonds that transcend individual challenges. Within these nurturing environments, the collective strength of Muslim communities shines brightest, offering respite from external pressures and reinforcing the community's endurance.

Empowerment Through Education

Recognizing the transformative potential of knowledge, Muslim Americans participate in educational endeavors designed to dismantle ignorance and prejudice. Through targeted initiatives, they endeavor to debunk misconceptions, confront stereotypes, and cultivate mutual understanding across diverse communities. Empowered by accurate insights into Islam and Muslims, individuals strive to combat entrenched biases and cultivate empathy and inclusivity. By equipping themselves and others with factual information, they embark on a journey to challenge negative perceptions and foster a climate of respect and acceptance. Through education, Muslim Americans endeavor to sow the seeds of empathy, nurturing a culture of understanding and unity in the face of division and discord.

Cultural & Artistic Expression

Harnessing the potency of creativity, Muslim artists, writers, musicians, and poets employ their talents to process emotions and translate collective anguish into poignant expressions. Through various artistic media, they amplify marginalized voices, share compelling narratives, and advocate for transformative social changes. They engage in cultural and creative endeavors to provide catharsis, promote toughness, and inspire optimism. By harnessing the power of creativity, Muslim individuals understand the complexities of their experiences, forging paths toward healing, empowerment, and societal transformation.

Community Advocacy & Activism

Turning frustration into fuel for change, Muslim Americans engage in advocacy and activism. They endeavor to confront systemic injustices and foster meaningful transformation. Through grassroots organizing, voter mobilization efforts, legislative advocacy, and community outreach initiatives, individuals amplify their voices and challenge discriminatory policies. They strive to advocate for social, economic, and political empowerment with unshakable determination. They work tirelessly to dismantle barriers, cultivate inclusivity, and advance equity. By harnessing their collective strength and mobilizing for change, Muslim Americans stand at the forefront of efforts to create a more just, equitable, and inclusive society for all.

Spiritual Strength

For countless Muslim Americans, faith and spirituality serve as steadfast anchors in the tumult of life, offering solace, direction, and absolute sturdiness in times of uncertainty. Individuals tap into the profound reservoir of their faith by engaging in prayer, introspection, and adherence to religious tenets. They discover inner peace, clarity of purpose, and a profound sense of belonging within their community and the broader world. Grounded in their spiritual convictions, they face the complexities of existence with resolve. They draw strength from their connection to the divine and find solace in knowing they are part of a larger, transcendent reality. Through their faith, Muslim Americans find sustenance, guidance, and a sense of purpose that sustains them through life's trials and tribulations.

Interfaith Collaboration

Muslim Americans participate in interfaith dialogue and collaboration to bridge religious and cultural divides, foster mutual understanding, and cultivate cooperation. By forging alliances with individuals from diverse backgrounds, they endeavor to combat bigotry, advocate for social justice, and cultivate inclusive communities where everyone is valued and respected. Through meaningful engagement and collaboration, Muslim Americans work alongside allies to dismantle barriers, promote empathy, and create spaces. Differences are celebrated, not feared or marginalized. In this spirit of unity and cooperation, they strive to build a more inclusive society where mutual respect and understanding are the foundation for a brighter, more harmonious future.

Pathways to Prosperity: Long-Term Solutions for Quality-of-Life Enhancement

Enhancing the long-term quality of life for Muslim Americans requires a multifaceted approach that addresses systemic inequalities, promotes social inclusion, and fosters holistic well-being. It necessitates a concerted effort from various stakeholders, including policymakers, community leaders, advocacy groups, and individuals within the community. Central to this endeavor is recognizing Muslim Americans' diverse needs and experiences, encompassing economic, social, cultural, and healthcare dimensions. The advocacy for policy change is at the forefront of efforts to improve long-term quality of life. This change entails lobbying for legislation that safeguards civil rights, combats discrimination, and promotes equal opportunities for all individuals. By advocating for policies that address systemic injustices and socioeconomic disparities, they can work toward creating a more equitable society where everyone has the opportunity to thrive.

Investment in education is another critical component of improving Muslim Americans' long-term quality of life. Providing access to quality education, promoting cultural competence in schools, and supporting higher education and vocational training programs are essential for empowering Muslim American youth and adults to achieve their full potential. Promoting economic empowerment is also paramount for enhancing long-term quality of life. This enhancement involves creating pathways for entrepreneurship, job training programs, and access to capital to overcome barriers to financial stability.

Furthermore, cultural integration and community-building initiatives are essential for nurturing Muslim Americans' sense of belonging and connectedness. This process includes promoting interfaith dialogue, celebrating cultural diversity, and organizing community events that unite people across religious and cultural divides. Access to healthcare and mental health services is also critical for improving long-term quality of life.

Ultimately, improving the long-term quality of life for Muslim Americans requires a collaborative effort. This collaboration must address the community's diverse needs and promote equity, inclusion, and opportunity for all. By working together to address systemic barriers and promote social, economic, and cultural empowerment, Muslim Americans can build a brighter future for themselves and future generations.

Chapter 8
Unraveling Tensions – Latin American Perspectives

The history of wars and territorialism of countries such as Cuba, Puerto Rico, or Mexico and oppressive regimes in Guatemala, El Salvador, Nicaragua, and the Dominican Republic has led to Latin Americans being the largest minority group in the country. The population of Hispanics in the U.S. sits at 62.5 million, an increase from 22.4 million in 1980 (Gonzalez, 2022; Moslimani & Noe-Bustamante, 2023). Although mass immigration was tied to the historic relations of the U.S. and Latin America, it was a process of labor importation for many. The mass immigration of Latin Americans has led to the involuntary creation of distinct ethnic minority groups, such as Mexican Americans and Puerto Ricans, many caused by exploitation and occupation of their countries. Many Latin Americans born in the U.S. continue to have strong bonds with their home countries and maintain social networks of kin, creating channels for future immigration. Despite being one of the largest ethnic minority groups in the country, many of them suffer from challenges such as discrimination, prejudice, or racism.

Despite these challenges, Latin American communities have a profound sense of power and solidarity. Drawing from centuries of indigenous wisdom and spiritual practices, individuals and families have developed coping mechanisms and support networks that transcend borders and generations. Through rituals, storytelling, and communal gatherings, they find solace and strength in their shared experiences, ensuring a sense of belonging and collective healing. As I present the complexities of mental struggles through the eyes of Latin Americans, I request that readers challenge preconceived notions, confront systemic inequalities, and advocate for more inclusive and culturally sensitive approaches to mental health care.

Sorrow & Disbelief

As we decipher the reality of the mental struggles of Latin Americans, we encounter narratives of sorrow and disbelief that weigh heavily on each soul that has endured them. Within the fabric of everyday life, shadows of anguish, despair, and profound sadness lurk beneath the vibrant colors of cultural celebration. In the quiet corners of homes and bustling streets alike, whispers of disbelief echo in the hearts of those with the overwhelming weight of their inner turmoil. Feelings of inadequacy, unworthiness, and hopelessness grip their minds, shrouding their perceptions of self and reality in a veil of darkness. Each day becomes a battle against the relentless onslaught of negative thoughts and emotions, eroding their sense of purpose and robbing them of joy. Like a relentless storm, heartbreak ravages the mind, leaving shards of shattered dreams and unfulfilled promises. It manifests in the silent tears of those who mourn the loss of loved ones to the silent epidemic of mental illness, their grief compounded by the stigma and misunderstanding that shroud the topic of mental health in secrecy and shame.

Anger simmers beneath the surface, a volatile force born of frustration, injustice, and the relentless struggle against unseen adversaries. It manifests in moments of explosive rage and simmering resentment, a testament to the profound sense of injustice and helplessness that permeates the lives of those marginalized by societal norms and systemic inequalities.

Anxiety, like an unrelenting specter, casts a long shadow over the lives of individuals grappling with the uncertainty of tomorrow. It manifests in the racing heartbeat, the clammy palms, and the gnawing sense of dread accompanying each step forward. Each decision is made in the face of an uncertain future.

Amid disbelief and sorrow, the spirit of Latin Americans remains intact. According the ones that I have assessed, they have witnessed the flickering flame of hope that refuses to be extinguished. Whether feeling sad over the lie of America being the greatest nation in the world or happy about the ray that shines regardless is a question that has left most befuddled.

Stereotypes & Fears

Latin Americans have long been subjected to harmful stereotypes and unjustified fears perpetuated by a combination of historical biases, cultural misconceptions, and systemic inequalities. These stereotypes often portray Latin Americans in a negative light, reinforcing stereotypes that are rooted in xenophobia, racism, and misinformation. Common stereotypes against Latin Americans include perceptions of being lazy, uneducated, or prone to criminal behavior. These stereotypes not only perpetuate harmful misconceptions but also contribute to discrimination, marginalization, and limited opportunities for Latin American individuals and communities. Many face the fear of being targeted as undocumented immigrants or border crossers, particularly in the context of immigration debates in countries like the U.S. These fears are compounded by policies and rhetoric that scapegoat Latin American immigrants, contributing to a climate of fear, mistrust, and hostility.

It is essential to recognize the damaging impact of stereotypes and fears against Latin Americans and work toward dismantling these harmful narratives. However, some stereotypes and fears have haunted the minds of countless Latin Americans, which are discussed in this section.

Stereotypes

Hot-Tempered or Passionate

Latin Americans are often unfairly portrayed as individuals who are hot-tempered or excessively passionate, with their emotions boiling over at the slightest provocation. This stereotype fails to acknowledge the rich cultural expression and emotional depth of Latin American communities. Although Latin American cultures embrace vibrant expressions of emotion, from lively celebrations to heartfelt expressions of love and solidarity, this aspect should not be misconstrued as impulsiveness or uncontrollable anger. Latin Americans are passionate about their beliefs, traditions, and values, but this passion is not synonymous with a lack of self-control or rationality. Instead, it reflects a deep-seated connection to their cultural heritage and a strong sense of identity.

Criminal or Violent

Latin Americans are unjustly stigmatized as inherently criminals or prone to violence, perpetuating harmful stereotypes that have real-world consequences for individuals and communities. This stereotype is rooted in historical and societal biases that paint Latin Americans as dangerous or threatening, contributing to systemic discrimination and marginalization. Nonetheless, if we look at the reality, Latin American communities are diverse and multifaceted, with law-abiding individuals who contribute positively to society in various ways. By perpetuating the stereotype of Latin Americans as criminals or violent, society overlooks the complex social, economic, and political factors that contribute to crime and violence in any community. Furthermore, this stereotype ignores the strength exhibited by these communities during agonizing periods, as well as their efforts to address underlying issues, such as poverty, inequality, and lack of access to resources.

Unskilled Laborers

The stereotype of Latin Americans as unskilled laborers perpetuates harmful misconceptions about the capabilities and contributions of individuals from such backgrounds. This stereotype ignores their diverse talents, skills, and expertise across various fields, from medicine and engineering to education and entrepreneurship. Latin American communities boast a vibrant innovation, creativity, and perseverance history. However, their stereotype as mere unskilled laborers, undermines their accomplishments and potential. By pigeonholing Latin Americans into low-skilled labor jobs, this stereotype perpetuates inequality and restricts opportunities for upward mobility and advancement. Latin American individuals excel in various professions and industries, making valuable contributions to their communities and U.S. society.

Illegal Immigrants or Border Crossers

The stereotype of Latin Americans as illegal immigrants or border crossers is deeply rooted in xenophobia, racism, and misinformation. This stereotype unfairly portrays Latin American immigrants as criminals or threats to national security, overlooking the diverse reasons why individuals migrate and the contributions they make to their new communities. However, the reality is quite different. Latin American immigrants come to the U.S. in search of better opportunities, fleeing poverty, violence, and persecution in their home countries. This stereotype ignores the long history of U.S. intervention in Latin America, including political destabilization, economic exploitation, and military intervention, which have contributed to the conditions that drive migration.

Ignorant or Backward

The stereotype of Latin Americans as ignorant or backward is a harmful misconception that undermines the rich cultural heritage and intellectual contributions of these communities. This stereotype perpetuates colonialist attitudes that paint Latin Americans as primitive or uncivilized, ignoring the vibrant traditions, art, literature, and scientific advancements that have emerged from Latin America. Latin American cultures have long histories of intellectual inquiry, innovation, and creativity, contributing to literature, philosophy, mathematics, and the sciences. The stereotype often overshadows the achievements and accomplishments of individuals from Latin American backgrounds and perpetuates harmful stereotypes that contribute to discrimination and marginalization. Moreover, the stereotype ignores the systemic barriers and opportunities for Latin Americans, perpetuating cycles of poverty and exclusion.

Exploring Fears

Discrimination

Latin Americans may harbor deep-seated fears of facing discrimination or prejudice rooted in their ethnicity, culture, or language. This fear permeates various aspects of their lives, infiltrating realms such as employment, education, housing, and interactions with law enforcement. In the workplace, Latin Americans may fear being overlooked for opportunities or promotions due to stereotypes or biases held by employers or colleagues. In school environments, people may expect to face hurdles to academic performance, social acceptance, and institutional disparities. In housing markets, they may face discrimination in rental or homeownership processes, leading to housing insecurity and instability. Interactions with law enforcement can also evoke profound apprehension, as Latin Americans fear being unfairly targeted or mistreated based on racial profiling or cultural stereotypes. These pervasive fears of discrimination not only erode individual well-being and sense of belonging but also perpetuate cycles of inequality and injustice within society.

Violence

Latin Americans grapple with profound fears of violence, both within their communities and at the hands of external threats. This pervasive fear is deeply rooted in lived experiences of crime and insecurity, as well as broader societal perceptions of Latin American communities as dangerous or prone to violence. Within their neighborhoods, Latin Americans may fear becoming victims of crime, with streets plagued by gang activity, drug-related violence, and interpersonal conflicts. This constant threat of violence casts a shadow over their daily lives, instilling a sense of vulnerability and hypervigilance. Moreover, they may fear violence perpetrated by external actors, including hate crimes, xenophobic attacks, or state-sanctioned violence. These fears not only impact individual well-being but also contribute to a climate of fear, mistrust, and social fragmentation within Latin American communities, perpetuating cycles of trauma and insecurity.

Immigration Enforcement

Latin Americans, particularly undocumented immigrants, grapple with profound fears of immigration enforcement, including deportation or separation from their families. These fears are exacerbated by aggressive immigration enforcement policies that target Latin American communities, instilling a pervasive sense of uncertainty and dread. Undocumented immigrants may live in continual dread of being detected and deported, creating an environment plagued with worry, tension, and secrecy. This fear of immigration enforcement undermines individual well-being and hinders access to essential services, such as healthcare, education, and legal assistance. Moreover, it perpetuates a climate of fear and mistrust within Latin American communities, discouraging individuals from reporting crimes or seeking help when needed. These fears of immigration enforcement underscore the urgent need for comprehensive immigration reform and compassionate policies that uphold the dignity and rights of all individuals, regardless of their immigration statuses.

Social Exclusion

Latin Americans experience profound fears of social exclusion or marginalization stemming from discrimination based on race, ethnicity, gender, sexual orientation, or socioeconomic status. These fears permeate various aspects of their lives, from interpersonal relationships to access to opportunities and resources. Latin Americans may fear being overlooked or dismissed in social or professional settings where their identities are invalidated or erased. Moreover, due to systemic inequalities and biases, they may face barriers to accessing essential services such as healthcare, education, or housing. This fear of social exclusion not only erodes individual well-being and self-esteem but also perpetuates cycles of marginalization and inequality within society. It underscores the urgent need for inclusive and equitable policies that address systemic barriers and promote diversity, belonging, and social cohesion.

Loss of Rights & Liberties

The constant fear of their rights and liberties, such as freedom of expression, assembly, and association, is also being eroded for Latin Americans. This pervasive fear is deeply rooted in historical and contemporary struggles against authoritarian regimes, censorship, surveillance, and threats to democratic institutions and civil liberties. Latin Americans may fear the curtailing of their freedom of expression, facing censorship or repression for speaking out against injustice or advocating for social change. This fear is compounded by the proliferation of surveillance technologies and the targeting of activists, journalists, and dissenting voices by state authorities or nonstate actors. Latin Americans also fear restrictions on their freedom of assembly and association, anticipating crackdowns on peaceful protests, social movements, and civil society organizations. This fear of loss of rights and liberties undermines individual autonomy and democratic principles and threatens the fabric of society, stifling dissent, innovation, and social progress. It underscores the urgent need for robust legal protections, democratic reforms, and vigilant advocacy efforts to safeguard the rights and liberties of all Latin Americans, ensuring that they can live in dignity, freedom, and justice.

Aftermath of Recent Occurrences – Border Crisis

The recent border crisis along the Mexico border from Texas to California intensified in May 2023, has had profound and far-reaching effects on Latin American communities, escalating existing fears and vulnerabilities while generating new challenges and uncertainties. Latin Americans confront a complex web of fears and anxieties stemming from the border crisis, encompassing concerns related to immigration policies, human rights violations, family separation, and humanitarian emergencies. The border crisis has intensified fears of immigration enforcement and deportation, particularly among undocumented immigrants and asylum seekers fleeing violence, persecution, and economic hardship in their home countries. Latin American families grapple with the agonizing prospect of separation, forced to deal with a treacherous journey to the U.S. border in search of safety and opportunity, only to face detention, deportation, or indefinite family separation. The border crisis has exacerbated fears of human rights violations and abuses, including reports of overcrowded detention facilities, inadequate access to medical care, and instances of violence and mistreatment at the hands of immigration authorities. Latin Americans confront the harrowing reality of being denied basic dignity and rights, subjected to dehumanizing conditions and arbitrary detention, with little recourse or legal protection.

Furthermore, the border crisis has profound psychological and emotional impacts on Latin American communities, fueling feelings of fear, trauma, and uncertainty. Families torn apart by deportation or detention experience profound grief and loss, while those awaiting asylum hearings or immigration proceedings endure prolonged periods of anxiety, stress, and instability. Regarding the border crisis, Latin American communities demonstrate remarkable unity, solidarity, and determination, mobilizing grassroots efforts to support migrants and advocate humane immigration policies. However, the long-term impacts of the border crisis on these communities remain uncertain, underscoring the urgent need for comprehensive and compassionate responses that uphold the dignity, rights, and humanity of all individuals, regardless of their immigration status or nationality.

Coping With Collective Anguish & Frustration

By exploring the emotional grounds of Latin American societies, we might discover how they can tackle mutual grief and dissatisfaction. Within the fabric of these societies, systemic injustices, sociopolitical unrest, and historical traumas intersect to shape the complexity of collective experience. From the streets of bustling urban centers to the remote corners of rural villages, Latin Americans display a spectrum of emotions oscillating among sorrow, anger, determination, and hope. If we dive deeper into collective anguish, there lies the weight of intergenerational trauma inherited from centuries of colonization, exploitation, and marginalization.

Latin Americans carry the scars of their ancestors, whose lives were marked by displacement, violence, and dispossession. These unresolved wounds manifest in contemporary struggles for justice, dignity, and equality, fueling a collective yearning for recognition, restitution, and reconciliation. Frustration simmers beneath the surface, a potent brew of discontent brewed from the inequities and injustices that pervade Latin American societies. From political corruption and economic inequality to environmental degradation and social exclusion, Latin Americans confront a litany of challenges that test the limits of their patience and resolve. Despite the chaos, there is a calm resolve to overcome despair and restore agency.

Latin Americans cope with collective anguish and frustration through myriad strategies reflecting the richness and diversity of their cultural heritage. They harness diverse avenues, including grassroots activism, community mobilization, artistic creativity, and inner strength, to understand the complexities of their daily lives. Through various forms of artistic expression, such as visual arts, music, and literature, they articulate their hardships, channeling pain into poetic creations, anger into activism, and despair into renewed hope. Solidarity is a beacon of light in the darkness, binding Latin American communities in their shared quest for justice and dignity.

Regardless of the situation for Latin Americans, a few sustainable strategies can be explored to enhance their long-term quality of life. Recognizing their multifaceted challenges, from economic inequality and social exclusion to environmental degradation and political instability, we seek to identify holistic approaches that promote lasting impact. Central to this exploration is a focus on addressing systemic inequalities and barriers to opportunity that perpetuate cycles of poverty and marginalization. Furthermore, the importance of participatory governance structures that amplify the voices of marginalized groups and ensure their needs are addressed in decision-making processes is also something that can be explored. By promoting transparency, accountability, and democratic participation, we can work toward creating a more just and equitable society where all individuals are given the opportunity to thrive. In addition to structural reforms, we recognize the importance of investing in social and cultural capital and nurturing networks of support and solidarity that strengthen social cohesion. By promoting cultural preservation, community engagement, and intergenerational knowledge-sharing, society can build a sense of belonging and identity that transcends borders and fosters collective well-being. The following section details ways to long-term prosperity with the aim of comprehending how society can help Latin American communities in this quest.

Pathways to Sustainable Long-Term Prosperity

Investing in Infrastructure & Public Services

Investing in infrastructure and public services is a pivotal step toward advancing the well-being and prosperity of Latin American communities. By committing resources to bolstering essential infrastructure, such as transportation networks, water supply systems, and sanitation facilities, governments lay the groundwork for sustainable development and improved quality of life. Reliable infrastructure facilitates the efficient movement of goods and people and ensures access to basic amenities essential for human dignity and well-being. Enhancing access to critical public services like healthcare and education is paramount to ensure social development and reduce disparities. Adequate healthcare infrastructure, including hospitals, clinics, and medical personnel, is indispensable for addressing public health challenges and ensuring access to essential healthcare services for all members of society.

Similarly, investing in education infrastructure, such as schools, libraries, and educational resources, is vital for nurturing human capital, empowering individuals, and giving rise to social mobility. These investments enhance the quality of life, stimulate economic growth, attract investment, and create opportunities for employment and entrepreneurship. By promoting inclusive and sustainable development, governments can strengthen external shocks and ensure the well-being of current and future generations.

Promoting Economic Diversification & Sustainable Growth

Encouraging economic diversification beyond conventional sectors like agriculture and mining is pivotal for robust, inclusive economies in the U.S. By broadening the economic base to include emerging industries such as technology, renewable energy, and tourism, the government can unlock new avenues for job creation, innovation, and prosperity. Additionally, prioritizing sustainable growth practices that balance economic development with environmental conservation and social equity is imperative for long-term economic stability. Embracing sustainable practices in resource extraction, manufacturing, and energy production minimizes environmental degradation and strengthens climate change and natural disasters.

Empowering Women & Advancing Gender Equality

Advancing gender equality and empowering women are critical steps toward enhancing Latin America's long-term quality of life. By dismantling barriers to women's education, economic participation, and political representation, societies can harness the immense potential of half their population, driving forward inclusive and sustainable development agendas. Addressing barriers to women's education ensures equal opportunities for all. By providing girls and women access to quality education, Latin American countries can equip them with the skills, knowledge, and confidence to pursue their aspirations and contribute meaningfully to society.

Moreover, investing in educational initiatives targeting girls and women from marginalized communities can help bridge gender gaps in educational attainment and promote social mobility. Moreover, promoting women's economic participation is essential for unlocking economic growth and reducing poverty. By addressing discriminatory practices in the labor market, providing access to credit and financial services, and supporting women entrepreneurs, societies can tap into a vast reservoir of talent and innovation. Furthermore, implementing policies that promote work-life balance, such as affordable childcare and parental leave, can enable women to participate in the workforce while fulfilling their caregiving responsibilities fully.

Enhancing Social Protection & Safety Nets

Bolstering social protection programs and safety nets is critical for providing vital support to vulnerable populations amidst periods of crisis and uncertainty. By broadening access to social assistance, healthcare coverage, and unemployment benefits, governments can play a pivotal role in alleviating the impacts of poverty and inequality while implementing greater social inclusion and determination. Expanding access to social assistance programs ensures that vulnerable individuals and families can acquire essential resources during times of need. By providing financial aid, food assistance, and housing support, these programs can help mitigate the immediate effects of economic hardship, safeguarding individuals from poverty and promoting their overall well-being.

Christopher A. Lowery, DHSc, CLCP

Chapter 9

Threads of Resilience – Native Americans & Other Racial Groups

The plight of Native Americans in the U.S. is a tragic narrative deeply ingrained in the fabric of American history. For centuries, Indigenous peoples have endured a relentless assault on their cultures, lands, and identities, resulting in profound intergenerational trauma and lasting mental health challenges. From the earliest days of European colonization to the present, Native Americans have faced displacement, genocide, forced assimilation, and systemic discrimination. The devastating consequences of these injustices continue to reverberate through Native communities, manifesting in alarmingly high rates of depression, anxiety, substance abuse, and suicide. The loss of ancestral lands and disruption of traditional ways of life have left many Native Americans grappling with feelings of profound grief, disconnection, and existential despair. The deliberate erasure of Indigenous languages, cultures, and spiritual practices has severed vital connections to identity and heritage, exacerbating feelings of cultural alienation and loss.

Moreover, the ongoing marginalization and neglect of Native communities perpetuate cycles of poverty, unemployment, and inadequate access to essential resources, such as healthcare and education. Historical trauma, compounded by contemporary social and economic disparities, creates a toxic brew of stress, hopelessness, and despair that exacts a heavy toll on Native mental well-being. The legacy of colonialism and institutional racism casts a long shadow over the mental health of Indigenous peoples. Structural barriers to healthcare, limited access to culturally competent services, and pervasive stereotypes and stigma surrounding mental illness further exacerbate the challenges faced by Native Americans seeking support and treatment. Along with these systemic challenges, Native communities also contend with environmental injustices, including the devastating impact of extractive industries on tribal lands, which contribute to feelings of powerlessness, anger, and environmental grief. The loss of traditional livelihoods and the degradation of sacred lands further compound the psychological toll of colonization and exploitation.

The historical experiences of the Native Americans, including forced assimilation, urbanizations, epidemics, and other restrictions, have led to various health disparities among this population. Many Natives rely on Food Distribution Programs due to their forced removal and land restriction (Blue Bird Jernigan et al., 2020). Many suffer from health issues caused by diabetes and obesity due to their restricted access to high-quality food. The psychological harm of colonization has led to significant trauma and mental health challenges for Native Americans. Many have questioned the psychological sense of belonging, especially with deconstructing their identity and losing their native language over time (King et al., 2019). They have experienced a historical disconnect due to forced urbanization, which caused a traumatic and distressing shift to a new reality.

Disbelief & Heartbreak

Disbelief and heartbreak are pervasive emotions deeply entrenched within the narrative of Native American struggles. These sentiments stem from centuries of enduring oppression, broken promises, and cultural genocide at the hands of colonial powers and subsequent governments. However, the disbelief arises from the stark contrast between the promises made to Indigenous peoples and the harsh realities they faced. From treaties that were systematically violated to policies of forced assimilation and relocation, Native communities have repeatedly been betrayed by those in positions of power. This betrayal has led to a profound sense of disillusionment and skepticism regarding the intentions of government entities and the dominant society.

Heartbreak permeates the collective consciousness of Native Americans as they bear witness to the ongoing loss of land, language, and cultural practices. The forced removal from ancestral homelands, the destruction of sacred sites, and the erosion of traditional knowledge evoke a deep sense of sorrow and mourning for what has been irretrievably lost. Moreover, the intergenerational trauma resulting from these injustices compounds the emotional anguish, perpetuating cycles of pain and suffering within Indigenous communities.

Disbelief and heartbreak intersect in the lived experiences of Native peoples, shaping their worldview and influencing their interactions with the broader society. These emotions serve as poignant reminders of the enduring legacy of colonialism and the ongoing struggle for justice, dignity, and self-determination. Despite their profound challenges, Native Americans continue to demonstrate strength. Their stories of survival, resistance, and cultural revitalization testify to the power of Indigenous determination and the enduring spirit of Native peoples in the ongoing quest for healing, justice, and reconciliation.

Stereotypes & Fears

Stereotypes and fears surrounding Native Americans have profound implications for their mental health and well-being. These harmful misconceptions perpetuate a climate of prejudice, discrimination, and marginalization, aggravating existing social and economic disparities and contributing to elevated rates of mental health challenges within Native communities. The pervasive stereotypes depicting Native Americans as primitive, violent, or exotic "others" serve to dehumanize and objectify them, eroding their sense of self-worth and identity. Constant exposure to these negative portrayals can lead to internalized racism, feelings of shame, and a diminished sense of belonging. These issues contribute to heightened levels of stress, anxiety, and depression among Native individuals.

Similarly, the fears and misconceptions of Native Americans as inherently dangerous or unpredictable can foster mistrust and hostility toward them, leading to experiences of discrimination, harassment, and violence. The threat of racial profiling, hate crimes, and institutionalized racism further compounds the psychological toll on Native communities, fueling feelings of fear, hypervigilance, and trauma. The erasure and misrepresentation of Native cultures, histories, and identities in mainstream media and educational curricula perpetuate feelings of cultural invisibility and alienation among Indigenous youth, undermining their sense of pride and connection to their heritage. This issue disconnects from cultural roots and traditions and can contribute to a sense of identity confusion, loss, and existential despair, further exacerbating mental health challenges among Native individuals.

Meaningless Stereotypes

Savage

This stereotype depicts Native Americans as inherently violent, uncivilized, and primitive, perpetuating the myth of the "savage warrior". This harmful depiction plays a massive role in minimizing the sophistication of Indigenous cultures and societies, reducing them to simplistic caricatures. By ignoring the rich histories, diverse traditions, and complex social structures of Native peoples, this stereotype perpetuates prejudice and discrimination against Indigenous communities. It erases their contributions to art, science, and literature while reinforcing harmful narratives of inferiority and barbarism.

Noble Savage

Native Americans are romanticized as mystical beings living harmoniously with nature. This idealization reduces them to simplistic and exoticized caricatures, overlooking the complexities of contemporary Indigenous life. With a portrayal of Native people as inherently virtuous and unspoiled by civilization, the realities of historical trauma, economic disparities, and cultural strength within Indigenous communities have been erased. It perpetuates harmful myths of primitivism and perpetuates a sense of otherness, further marginalizing Native voices and experiences.

Drunken Indian

The "Drunken Indian" stereotype portrays Native Americans as inherently prone to alcoholism and substance abuse. This harmful characterization overlooks the historical trauma and systemic factors that contribute to these issues within Native communities. By focusing on individual behaviors, this stereotype perpetuates misconceptions and stigma. It ignores the underlying socioeconomic disparities, lack of access to healthcare, and intergenerational trauma that contribute to substance abuse issues.

Casino Riches

It is often said that Native Americans are wealthy and financially successful solely due to casino gaming revenues. This oversimplified portrayal overlooks the economic challenges and disparities faced by many Indigenous peoples. Although some tribes have generated revenue from gaming enterprises, many Indigenous communities continue to grapple with poverty, unemployment, and inadequate access to essential resources. This stereotype perpetuates misconceptions about Native economic prosperity, ignoring the historical injustices, land dispossession, and ongoing socioeconomic barriers that hinder economic development and prosperity within Indigenous communities.

Mystical Shaman

Mystical clichés and oversimplified caricatures are common for this population. Native Americans are often portrayed as mystical shamans, which tends to take all focus from the cultural significance and diversity of Indigenous spiritual beliefs and practices, resulting in the complexities and richness of Native cosmologies and worldviews being erased. By fetishizing Native spirituality and presenting it as mysterious or supernatural, this stereotype perpetuates harmful myths of primitivism and a sense of otherness. It fails to recognize the deep spiritual connections to land, community, and ancestors that inform Indigenous belief systems. It overlooks the role of Indigenous spiritual leaders and practitioners as stewards of cultural knowledge and traditions. Challenging this stereotype requires acknowledging the diversity and complexity of Indigenous spiritualities, respecting the autonomy and sovereignty of Native communities, and initiating dialogue and understanding grounded in mutual respect and cultural humility.

Vanishing Race

The stereotype of Native Americans as a "Vanishing Race" is off-base. It is this idea that they are fading away like they are on the verge of disappearing altogether. However, that could not be further from the truth. Native American communities remain strong, alive with vibrant cultures and traditions. This stereotype makes it seem like they are relics of the past, which is an untrue narrative. Native peoples are still here, fighting for their rights and keeping their cultures alive. It is crucial to recognize the strength and endurance of Native communities while rejecting stereotypes that undermine their visibility and dignity.

Tormenting Fears

Cultural Erasure

Native Americans fear the loss of their cultural heritage and traditional ways of life due to centuries of assimilation efforts, cultural suppression policies, and the erosion of Indigenous languages, practices, and knowledge systems. The historical trauma of forced removal from ancestral lands, boarding school assimilation programs, and religious persecution has left deep scars on Native communities, contributing to a sense of cultural disconnection and loss. Moreover, the pervasive influence of mainstream Western culture and media often marginalizes Indigenous perspectives, perpetuating stereotypes and erasing Indigenous voices from public discourse. This fear of cultural erasure underscores the urgent need for cultural revitalization efforts, language preservation initiatives, and policies that respect and uphold Indigenous rights to self-determination and cultural sovereignty.

Land Dispossession

Throughout history, Native Americans continue to face the horrors of having their ancestral lands in the hands of government-sanctioned policies of land dispossession, forced removal, and resource extraction. From the devastating impacts of colonization and treaty violations to contemporary threats posed by land development, environmental degradation, and corporate exploitation, Native communities grapple with the constant threat of losing their sacred homelands and natural resources. This fear of land dispossession is compounded by the historical trauma of displacement, loss, and genocide, as well as ongoing legal battles over land rights and sovereignty. Addressing this fear requires honoring treaty agreements, upholding Indigenous land rights, and supporting land stewardship initiatives prioritizing Indigenous sovereignty and environmental justice.

Sovereignty Threats

The fear of threats to Native American tribal sovereignty, which includes their right to self-governance, cultural autonomy, and control over their lands and resources, is deeply concerning. Despite legal recognition of tribal sovereignty in the U.S., Native communities face ongoing challenges to their political and legal rights, including efforts to undermine tribal jurisdiction, restrict treaty rights, and erode tribal sovereignty through legislative and judicial actions. This fear of sovereignty threats is exacerbated by historical patterns of federal paternalism, assimilationist policies, and colonialist ideologies that seek to undermine Indigenous governance structures and tribal self-determination. Protecting tribal sovereignty requires upholding treaty obligations, respecting tribal governance systems, and supporting Indigenous—led efforts to reclaim and assert sovereignty over their lands, laws, and institutions.

Economic Insecurity

Many Native American communities face economic challenges stemming from historical injustices, systemic inequalities, and structural barriers to economic opportunity. High rates of poverty, unemployment, and lack of access to essential resources contribute to fears of economic insecurity and socioeconomic marginalization within Native communities. Historical trauma may include the legacy of forced removal from ancestral lands, the loss of traditional livelihoods, and discriminatory policies that hindered economic development. These issues have exacerbated economic disparities for Native peoples. Additionally, limited access to quality education, healthcare, and infrastructure further compounds the economic challenges faced by Native peoples. Addressing economic insecurity necessitates targeted investments in economic development initiatives, job training programs, and infrastructure projects that empower Native communities, promote self-sufficiency, and foster sustainable economic growth.

Health Disparities

Native Americans experience significant disparities in healthcare access, quality, and outcomes compared to the general population, leading to fears of inadequate medical care and poorer health outcomes. Historical traumas, including the legacy of colonization, forced assimilation, and intergenerational trauma, contribute to increased rates of chronic diseases, mental health disorders, and substance abuse within Native communities. Limited access to healthcare facilities, culturally competent care, and preventative services further exacerbates these health disparities. Additionally, environmental injustices, including exposure to pollution, inadequate sanitation, and lack of clean water, add to heightened health risks within Indigenous communities. Tackling these health disparities requires addressing the root causes of systemic inequalities, increasing access to quality healthcare services, and implementing culturally responsive public health interventions that prioritize Indigenous health needs and promote holistic wellness.

Environmental Degradation

Native American communities often reside in areas disproportionately affected by environmental pollution, resource extraction, and climate change. These issues lead to fears of environmental degradation, loss of traditional livelihoods, and threats to cultural and spiritual connections to the land. Historical patterns of colonization, land dispossession, and environmental racism have resulted in the disproportionate siting of toxic waste sites, industrial facilities, and extractive industries in or near Indigenous lands. These issues have exacerbated health risks and environmental injustices faced by Native peoples. Additionally, climate change poses existential threats to Indigenous communities, including sea-level rise, extreme weather events, and loss of biodiversity, further compromising their ability to sustain traditional ways of life. Addressing environmental degradation requires centering Indigenous knowledge, values, and sovereignty in environmental decision-making processes, supporting Indigenous-led conservation efforts, and advocating for policies prioritizing environmental justice and respecting Indigenous rights to land and natural resources.

Impact of Recent Events: Encroachment of Land

Recent events involving the encroachment of land have had profound and wide-ranging impacts on Native American communities. From the construction of pipelines and extractive industries to the expansion of urban development and agricultural projects, the encroachment of land threatens the sovereignty, culture, and livelihoods of Indigenous peoples. The encroachment of land often occurs without meaningful consultation or consent from affected Native communities, disregarding their rights to self-determination and stewardship over their ancestral territories. This lack of consultation not only violates legal obligations and treaty agreements but also undermines the spiritual and cultural significance of Indigenous lands, which are often considered sacred and integral to Indigenous identities. The encroachment of land poses significant environmental risks, including pollution, habitat destruction, and loss of biodiversity, which disproportionately impact Indigenous communities reliant on the land for subsistence, cultural practices, and traditional knowledge. Environmental degradation resulting from land encroachment exacerbates health disparities and undermines Indigenous sovereignty and self-sufficiency.

Moreover, the encroachment of land perpetuates cycles of economic dependency and socioeconomic marginalization within Native communities, as it restricts access to traditional resources, disrupts traditional livelihoods, and undermines economic opportunities for Indigenous peoples. Addressing the impact of recent events involving land encroachment requires upholding Indigenous rights to land and natural resources, respecting treaty obligations, and prioritizing meaningful consultation and consent processes that center Indigenous voices and perspectives. It also entails supporting Indigenous-led conservation efforts, sustainable land management practices, and initiatives that promote environmental justice and Indigenous sovereignty.

Coping With Shared Grief & Resentment

Coping with collective anguish and frustration poses an immense challenge for Native American communities. The enduring wounds of historical trauma, systemic oppression, and cultural erosion penetrate deep into the emotional and psychological fabric of Indigenous peoples, leaving indelible marks that reverberate across generations. This burden weighs heavily, manifesting in feelings of grief, anger, and despair as Native communities grapple with the relentless assault on their cultural identity and sovereignty. At its core, it is a struggle ingrained in the essence of Indigenous existence—a relentless battle to safeguard cultural identity and reclaim ancestral lands against insurmountable odds. The fight is woven into the fabric of Indigenous heritage, where endurance meets resistance. This ongoing battle is not just about reclaiming physical territories but also about preserving the soul of Indigenous cultures, resisting erasure, and asserting sovereignty in a world that often seeks to silence and diminish their voices.

In order to navigate this turbulent emotional landscape, Native communities lean on their intrinsic strength, cultural wisdom, and collective fortitude. They cultivate environments conducive to healing, grieving, and cultural rejuvenation, finding solace and empowerment in embracing their shared heritage. These spaces serve as sanctuaries, where the echoes of ancestral wisdom reverberate, strengthening community bonds. Indigenous peoples reclaim agency over their narratives through ceremonies, storytelling, and traditional practices. They forge pathways toward healing and renewal amidst the turbulence of their collective journey.

Nevertheless, the fight for justice and recognition is far from over. Native Americans continue to advocate for their rights, amplify their voices, and demand accountability from those who perpetuate injustice. It is a journey characterized by hardship, sacrifice, unity, and determination. Amidst the collective anguish and frustration, Native American communities stand resolute, anchored by the wisdom passed down through generations and inspired by the promise of a brighter future. They serve as stewards of a vibrant cultural heritage, protectors of sacred lands, and masters of their fate. Within their struggle resonates a profound message of fortitude, defiance, and the unyielding essence that defines Indigenous peoples worldwide. It is a testament to their commitment to uphold their legacy, safeguard their present, and forge ahead with tenacity, embodying the enduring spirit of Indigenous strength and perseverance. The following section details ways to long-term prosperity to better understand how society can help these communities.

Pathways to Sustainable Long-Term Prosperity

Improving the long-term quality of life for Native American communities necessitates comprehensive strategies that target the root causes of systemic inequalities while promoting sustainable growth and prosperity. Central to this endeavor is the recognition of the multifaceted challenges faced by Indigenous peoples, ranging from economic marginalization and inadequate access to education and healthcare to environmental degradation and loss of cultural heritage. Investing in education and vocational training programs is vital in breaking the cycle of poverty and empowering individuals within Native American communities. These initiatives enhance employability and cultivate a sense of agency and self-determination by equipping them with relevant skills and knowledge. Thus, participants gain the confidence to shape their futures and contribute meaningfully to their communities. These programs bridge traditional knowledge with modern industries and bring adaptability in dynamic economic environments. Ultimately, education investment creates pathways to prosperity, igniting hope and driving economic revitalization within Indigenous communities.

Furthermore, backing small businesses and entrepreneurship initiatives offers significant promise in rejuvenating local economies and establishing routes to economic autonomy within Indigenous communities. These efforts provide aspiring entrepreneurs with vital financial support, technical direction, and mentorship, providing innovation, employment opportunities, and economic stability. As a result, reliance on external income sources diminishes, nurturing self-reliance and bolstering economic sustainability. By nurturing a culture of entrepreneurship and enterprise, these programs empower individuals to cultivate their ventures, contribute to community prosperity, and chart a course toward self-determination and economic empowerment. Access to affordable healthcare services and infrastructure improvements are critical to long-term development strategies. By expanding healthcare coverage, improving healthcare infrastructure, and increasing culturally competent care, Indigenous communities can address health disparities, promote wellness, and enhance overall quality of life.

Emphasizing environmental conservation and renewable energy initiatives safeguards natural resources and resonates with Indigenous stewardship and sustainability principles. By melding traditional wisdom with contemporary conservation strategies, Native communities uphold their ancestral lands, safeguard biodiversity, and mitigate the effects of climate change for posterity. This fusion of knowledge and application respects cultural heritage and secures the long-term sustainability of ecosystems, conserving vital resources and preserving adaptability in confronting environmental challenges. Through these efforts, Indigenous communities assert their roles as guardians of the land and architects of a sustainable future.

The path to long-term improvement in the quality of life for Native communities lies in holistic solutions that empower individuals, foster self-sufficiency, and honor cultural heritage and sovereignty. By prioritizing Indigenous voices, values, and perspectives in the design and execution of development initiatives, policymakers can ensure inclusivity, equity, and sustainability. This approach tackles systemic challenges, cultivates adaptability, and paves the way for a prosperous future. By embracing Indigenous solutions, society may lay the groundwork for a more vibrant and resilient future for all Indigenous peoples.

Chapter 10
Unraveling Tensions – Asian Americans

Asian Americans have played an integral role in shaping the diverse fabric of American society, enriching it with their cultural heritage and bolstering its economic prosperity. However, their path has been marred by many challenges spanning generations. Rooted in historical discrimination, systemic barriers, and enduring stereotypes, the struggles faced by Asian Americans are complex and multifaceted. From the implementation of discriminatory laws such as the Chinese Exclusion Act to the internment of Japanese Americans during World War II, institutionalized racism has hindered their full integration into American life. Moreover, the pervasive model minority myth has obscured the socioeconomic disparities within the community, placing undue pressure on individuals to conform to unrealistic standards of success. These societal pressures often contribute to mental health issues, such as anxiety, depression, and feelings of inadequacy among Asian Americans.

Despite advancements in education and professional attainment, Asian Americans continue to confront systemic barriers, such as the bamboo ceiling in corporate America and limited representation in leadership roles. Additionally, language barriers, cultural differences, and health disparities further compound the challenges they face. In recent years, the alarming rise in anti-Asian racism and hate crimes has underscored the urgency of addressing these issues and providing a more inclusive society. Despite these obstacles, Asian Americans pursue equality and acceptance, advocating for meaningful change and contributing to the ongoing narrative of America's diverse culture.

Impact of Perpetual Foreignness & Pandemic Stressors

Perpetual Foreignness

Perpetual foreignness is a concept deeply ingrained in the experiences of Asian Americans, representing the persistent perception of individuals as outsiders, regardless of their citizenship or generational status. This enduring stereotype undermines their sense of belonging and perpetuates feelings of alienation and marginalization within American society. Despite their significant contributions to various aspects of American life, Asian Americans continue to encounter microaggressions, discrimination, and stereotyping based on their racial or ethnic background. This perpetual foreignness not only erodes their self-esteem but also creates formidable barriers to social integration and professional advancement, hindering their ability to fully participate in and benefit from the opportunities afforded by society.

Consequently, many Asian Americans grapple with a profound sense of disconnection from their cultural identity and heritage. Their experiences are often invalidated or dismissed, further exacerbating feelings of isolation and cultural alienation. Addressing the pervasive impact of perpetual foreignness requires concerted efforts to challenge and dismantle stereotypes, foster greater inclusivity and belonging, and promote cultural understanding and appreciation within American society.

Pandemic Stressors

The COVID-19 pandemic has intensified the difficulties experienced by Asian Americans, exacerbating preexisting inequalities and amplifying feelings of vulnerability and insecurity within the community. Asian Americans have borne a disproportionate burden of the pandemic's impacts, facing economic and social challenges at heightened rates. The surge in anti-Asian sentiment and hate crimes has instilled widespread fear and anxiety, exacerbating stress and trauma among Asian Americans.

Additionally, the pandemic-induced isolation, financial strain, and health concerns have compounded existing mental health issues within the community, amplifying feelings of distress and uncertainty. As a result, many Asian Americans grapple with heightened levels of stress, anxiety, and depression, further complicating their ability to comprehend the challenges of daily life. Addressing the mental health implications of pandemic stressors among Asian Americans requires comprehensive efforts to provide accessible and culturally competent mental health support, dismantle xenophobic attitudes and behaviors, and foster a sense of community power and solidarity.

Addressing the Invisible Toll

The intersection of perpetual foreignness and pandemic stressors has profound implications for the mental health and well-being of Asian Americans. The persistent pressure to deal with multiple cultural identities, combined with the heightened fear of discrimination and social stigma, significantly contributes to increased rates of stress, anxiety, depression, and other psychological issues within the community. Moreover, cultural factors such as the stigma surrounding mental health, language barriers, and a scarcity of culturally competent resources may hinder Asian Americans from seeking help or accessing adequate support services. Consequently, many individuals grapple with their mental health challenges in silence, exacerbating their struggles and diminishing their overall quality of life.

Asian Americans have long been considered perpetual foreigners, making them particularly vulnerable to racism and discrimination. Historic events, such as the exclusion of this entire ethnic group during World War II, have left Asian Americans with traumatic memories of dehumanizing discrimination (Hahm et al., 2021). Until today, Asian Americans continue to be the subject of overt racism in the country; events such as workplace discrimination, harassment, or even violence remains common. Many continue to suffer from mental health problems, psychological distress, and even premature mortality. Many may even turn to *internalized racism*, which is where Asian Americans begin to accept the negative and racist messages about themselves and determine their worth accordingly. This battle has continued to affect millions of Asian Americans today.

Historical Injustices: Displacement & Enduring Discrimination

Chinese Exclusion Act (1882)

The Chinese Exclusion Act of 1882 was the first significant law restricting immigration into the U.S. It specifically targeted Chinese laborers, prohibiting their immigration for 10 years and barring those already in the country from becoming naturalized citizens. This act was driven by anti-Chinese sentiment fueled by economic competition and racial prejudice, particularly on the West Coast, where leaders perceived Chinese immigrants as a threat to White workers.

Japanese American Internment (1942–1945)

Following the attack on Pearl Harbor by Japan in 1941, President Franklin D. Roosevelt issued Executive Order 9066, which authorized the forced relocation and incarceration of over 120,000 Japanese Americans living on the West Coast. Despite most being U.S. citizens, they were deemed potential security risks solely based on their Japanese ancestry. Families were uprooted from their homes and livelihoods and forced into remote internment camps, where they endured harsh living conditions and loss of personal freedoms.

Asian Exclusion Acts (Various Dates)

Besides the Chinese Exclusion Act, several other legislative measures were implemented to restrict Asian immigration. For example, the Immigration Act of 1917 imposed a literacy test and a head tax, effectively barring immigration from Asia. The Immigration Act of 1924 established a national origins quota system, severely limiting immigration from Asian countries and perpetuating discriminatory practices.

Asian American Labor Exploitation

Asian immigrants, mainly Chinese and Filipino laborers, faced widespread exploitation and discrimination in the workplace. They were often relegated to low-paying, menial jobs such as railroad construction, agricultural labor, and domestic work. Moreover, they faced unsafe working conditions, long hours, and discriminatory practices by employers and labor unions, leading to economic exploitation and social marginalization.

Anti-Asian Violence & Massacres

Asian Americans were frequent targets of racial violence and targeted attacks throughout the late 19th and early 20th centuries. Incidents such as the Rock Springs Massacre in Wyoming in 1885, where Chinese miners were lynched and their homes destroyed by a White mob, and the Watsonville Riots in California in 1930, where White vigilantes attacked Filipino farmworkers, illustrate the prevalence of anti-Asian sentiment and violence during this period.

Exclusion From Citizenship & Legal Rights

Asian immigrants faced legal barriers to citizenship and were often denied fundamental rights and privileges afforded to other Americans. The Alien Land Laws, enacted in various states, prohibited Asian immigrants from owning land, leasing property, or establishing businesses in certain areas. Additionally, the Cable Act of 1922 revoked the citizenship of American women who married Asian immigrants, reinforcing racial hierarchies and perpetuating exclusionary practices.

Asian American Stereotyping & Discrimination

Asian Americans have long faced harmful stereotypes and discriminatory attitudes, perpetuating the perception of them as perpetual foreigners and reinforcing racial hierarchies. During times of economic hardship or public health crises, Asian communities have been scapegoated and targeted with discriminatory policies and acts of violence, such as the scapegoating of Chinese immigrants during the 19th-century economic downturns and the recent rise in anti-Asian hate crimes amid the COVID-19 pandemic. These stereotypes and discriminatory practices have contributed to the marginalization and social exclusion of Asian Americans within American society.

As we reflect on the deeply troubling history of Asian Americans in the U.S., we cannot overlook the profound mental struggles endured by individuals and communities affected by historical injustices, displacement, and enduring discrimination. The systematic targeting of Asian immigrants through discriminatory laws, such as the Chinese Exclusion Act and the Immigration Act of 1924, inflicted immeasurable psychological harm, with feelings of alienation, fear, and hopelessness. The forced relocation and incarceration of Japanese Americans during World War II shattered families and communities, leaving lasting scars on the collective psyche. Moreover, the persistent exclusion from citizenship and legal rights, coupled with widespread anti-Asian violence and discrimination, compounded the mental anguish experienced by Asian Americans throughout history. These injustices have left a legacy of trauma and psychological distress that continues to reverberate through generations, impacting individuals' sense of identity, belonging, and well-being.

Anguish & Reassessment of Identity Amid Racial Divides & Incorporating Anger Management Research

Due to the complexity of racial divides and societal pressures, Asian Americans often find themselves grappling with profound anguish and a reassessment of identity. The experience of discrimination, marginalization, and stereotyping can profoundly impact individuals' sense of self-worth and belonging, leading to internal turmoil and existential questioning. Moreover, the enduring legacy of historical injustices and systemic racism exacerbates these struggles, amplifying feelings of anger, frustration, and disillusionment. As they confront these challenges, Asian Americans are compelled to confront not only the external pressures of discrimination but also the internal struggle to reconcile their identities in a society that often fails to fully acknowledge their humanity. This ongoing battle against racial injustice and societal expectations underscores the urgent need for support and resources to address the mental health and well-being of Asian American communities.

Harnessing Strength: Empowering Asian American Communities Through Anger Management & Cultural Determination

Incorporating insights from anger management research becomes imperative in addressing these challenges and providing strength within Asian American communities. By providing individuals with tools and strategies to manage and channel their emotions effectively, we can empower them to face hardship with grace and grit. Moreover, promoting a deeper understanding of identity formation and cultural heritage can facilitate a sense of belonging and strengthen community bonds. As Asian Americans confront the complexities of racial discrimination and societal expectations, it becomes increasingly crucial to equip them with the necessary skills and resources to face these challenges. Through evidence-based practices and culturally sensitive approaches, we can empower individuals to assert their identities confidently and advocate for their rights within society.

As we confront the complexities of racial divides and societal pressures, it is essential to prioritize the mental well-being of Asian Americans and provide them with the support and resources needed to deal with these challenges. By embracing a holistic approach that integrates anger management research with cultural sensitivity and identity affirmation, we can empower Asian Americans to reclaim their narratives, cultivate power, and thrive during challenging circumstances. Recognizing the unique challenges faced by Asian American communities, it is imperative to develop tailored interventions that address the intersectionality of their experiences, incorporating culturally sensitive practices and resources. By creating safe spaces for dialogue and healing, we can foster a sense of belonging and solidarity within Asian American communities, enabling individuals to confront systemic injustices with determination. Moreover, by promoting greater awareness and understanding of the diverse experiences and contributions of Asian Americans, we can challenge stereotypes and promote social inclusion and equity. In doing so, we can create a more just and compassionate society where all individuals are valued, respected, and supported in their journeys toward holistic well-being.

Addressing Anger Within Cultural Identity Struggles

Addressing anger within cultural identity struggles is a crucial endeavor that demands a comprehensive understanding of the intricate psychological dynamics at play within Asian American communities. Many individuals within these communities, grapple with intense feelings of anger stemming from their encounters with discrimination, marginalization, and the immense pressure to reconcile and understand the intricacies of their multifaceted cultural identities. This anger may surface from a profound sense of injustice, overwhelming frustration, and the internal turmoil of juggling and reconciling multiple cultural expectations.

Regarding cultural identity struggles, anger can manifest in myriad ways, ranging from deep-seated resentment toward societal norms to an acute frustration with pervasive stereotypes. Furthermore, it can lead to internal strife and conflict within familial or community dynamics. The suppression or mishandling of this anger can further compound the issue, resulting in the internalization of stress and emotional turmoil, as well as strained interpersonal relationships.

Effectively addressing anger within cultural identity struggles necessitates a multifaceted approach that acknowledges the intersectionality of individuals' experiences. This approach involves establishing safe and inclusive spaces where individuals can freely express and process their emotions, ensuring that their experiences are validated and respected. Furthermore, it requires providing culturally sensitive support and resources tailored to the unique needs of Asian American communities. Moreover, creating a deeper understanding of cultural identity formation and encouraging self-reflection are pivotal in helping individuals understand the complexities of their identities and cultivate healthier coping mechanisms for managing anger.

By undertaking these efforts, we can empower individuals to confidently embrace their authentic selves, assert their identities, and gracefully face the challenges of cultural assimilation. Through open dialogue, educational initiatives, and robust community support systems, we can create a more inclusive and nurturing environment where individuals feel empowered to confront and address the multifaceted layers of their cultural identities and experiences, giving a sense of belonging and collective empowerment within Asian American communities. Therefore, the following section discusses coping mechanisms and strategies for addressing this anger.

Coping Mechanisms & Strategies for Managing Anger

The complexities of cultural identity struggles, often entail confronting and managing intense feelings of anger that stem from experiences of discrimination, marginalization, and the pressure to reconcile conflicting cultural expectations. In this context, it becomes imperative to explore coping mechanisms and strategies tailored to the unique needs of individuals within Asian American communities.

Cultivating Emotional Awareness

Encouraging individuals within Asian American communities to cultivate awareness of their emotions and the triggers that lead to feelings of anger is an essential initial step in managing anger. By creating a deeper understanding of their emotional responses, individuals can develop strategies to effectively tackle anger. This process involves introspection and reflection to recognize patterns and triggers that provoke anger reactions. Through this heightened self-awareness, individuals can implement techniques such as deep breathing, mindfulness practices, and assertive communication to address anger constructively. Nevertheless, open dialogues and sharing coping strategies have proven to be quite helpful in managing anger and promoting emotional well-being within Asian American communities.

Mindfulness & Meditation Practices

Introducing mindfulness and meditation practices can be instrumental in helping Asian American individuals regulate their emotions and cultivate a sense of inner calm amidst the storm of cultural identity struggles. Individuals can develop emotional stability by grounding themselves in the present moment and observing their thoughts and feelings without judgment. These practices enable individuals to step back from overwhelming emotions and gain perspective, allowing them to respond to challenges with clarity and composure. Moreover, mindfulness and meditation provide tools for managing stress and anxiety, which are often exacerbated by cultural identity struggles. Individuals can foster a deeper connection to themselves and cultivate a sense of peace amidst the complexities of their cultural identities by incorporating these practices into their daily routines.

Assertive Communication Skills

Assertive communication skills empower people to express feelings and concerns constructively and respectfully, which Asian American communities can benefit from. By initiating open and honest dialogue, individuals can better understand conflicts and address underlying issues contributing to feelings of anger within familial, social, and professional relationships. Assertive communication involves expressing oneself with confidence while respecting the perspectives of others, thus resulting in mutual understanding and resolution. Through assertive communication, individuals can assert their boundaries, clarify misunderstandings, and seek compromises, leading to healthier and more harmonious relationships. Moreover, these skills can help community members feel empowered to express themselves authentically and advocate for their needs.

Seeking Support Networks

Encouraging individuals within Asian American communities to seek supportive networks can provide invaluable emotional support and validation. Whether through peer support groups, cultural organizations, or counseling services, connecting with others who share similar experiences can foster a sense of solidarity and empowerment. These supportive networks offer a safe space for individuals to share their struggles, seek advice, and receive encouragement from those who understand their unique cultural challenges. By bringing a sense of belonging and community, these networks help individuals feel less isolated and more understood by alleviating anger and distress. Additionally, these networks can provide access to resources and information that can aid in understanding cultural identity struggles and managing emotions effectively. Cultivating supportive networks within Asian American communities strengthens bonds and enhances overall well-being.

Engaging in Self-Care Practices

Prioritizing self-care practices, such as exercise, creative expression, and relaxation techniques, can be vital in managing anger and promoting overall well-being within Asian American communities. Individuals can create balance amidst cultural identity struggles by nurturing physical, emotional, and spiritual health. Engaging in regular exercise not only releases endorphins but also provides an outlet for pent-up frustration and stress. Similarly, creative expression through art, music, or writing allows individuals to process their emotions and find catharsis. Additionally, relaxation techniques such as deep breathing, meditation, or yoga can help individuals center themselves and reduce feelings of anger and anxiety. Individuals can replenish their energy reserves, improve their mood, and enhance their ability to cope with the complexities of cultural identity struggles by incorporating these self-care practices into their routines. Ultimately, prioritizing self-care enables individuals to nurture their well-being holistically and face life's challenges with equilibrium.

Seeking Professional Guidance

Recognizing when professional guidance is needed is crucial in effectively managing anger within Asian American communities. Mental health professionals, counselors, or therapists with expertise in cultural competency can provide individuals with tailored support and therapeutic interventions to address underlying issues contributing to feelings of anger and distress. Seeking professional guidance offers individuals a safe and confidential space to explore their emotions, identify triggers, and develop coping strategies specific to their cultural context. Moreover, culturally competent professionals can understand the nuances of cultural identity struggles, and provide validation and support without judgment. Through therapy or counseling sessions, individuals can gain insight into their thought patterns and behaviors, learn healthy coping mechanisms, and work toward resolving underlying issues contributing to their anger.

By exploring and implementing coping mechanisms and strategies according to the unique experiences and needs of Asian American communities, society may empower individuals to manage anger effectively and address the complexities of cultural identity struggles with grace. Through a holistic approach that integrates awareness about how stereotypes can promote prejudice by speaking out, encouraging collective action, actively boycotting, and demanding accountability, individuals can cultivate greater emotional well-being and empowerment on their journey toward self-discovery and identity affirmation (Hwang, 2021).

Christopher A. Lowery, DHSc, CLCP

Chapter 11

Unraveling Tensions – Mexican Americans

Latin American refers to someone who is a descendent of any Latin American country, whereas Mexican American refers to someone who is a descendent of Mexico specifically. Mexican Americans make up the most significant Latino population in the U.S. (with a reported figure of 37.41 million in 2022; Statista, n.d.). The most significant contributor to the Latin American population in the U.S. is by birth. However, it is important to note that a substantial percentage of Latin Americans immigrate to the country every year. In 2022, the population in the U.S. had grown by 24.5 million, and the Latin American population accounted for 53% of that increase (Krogstad et al., 2023). Despite the growing immigration rates of Mexicans, the most extensive immigration period for this group was reported between 1970 and 1990 (Durand & Massey, 2019).

The experiences of Mexican Americans in the U.S. are profoundly complex and fraught with systemic challenges that have persisted for generations. From enduring discrimination and marginalization to grappling with socioeconomic disparities and immigration issues, they have faced a myriad of obstacles in their pursuit of the American Dream. Unequal access to education, healthcare, and economic opportunities continue to plague many Mexican American communities, perpetuating cycles of poverty and inequality. Additionally, pervasive stereotypes and xenophobia contribute to a hostile social climate that undermines their dignity and well-being. Addressing these struggles requires a comprehensive approach that tackles root causes while promoting inclusivity, equity, and social justice. By amplifying the voices of Mexican Americans, advocating for policy reforms, and increasing understanding and empathy, we can work toward building a more equitable and inclusive society where all individuals have the opportunity to thrive, regardless of their ethnic or cultural backgrounds.

Dual Cultural Pressures Along the Borders of America

Mexican Americans reside along the Mexican American borders or the inland boundary between Mexico and the U.S., which is indirectly on the coastline. They often grapple with the unique challenges of dual cultural pressures. Caught between two worlds, they face the daunting task of reconciling their Mexican heritage with the expectations and norms of mainstream American society. This duality can manifest from linguistic and cultural identity struggles to conflicting societal expectations and pressures. On one hand, Mexican Americans may feel a strong connection to their cultural roots, cherishing traditions, language, and customs passed down through generations. However, they may still encounter external pressures to assimilate into American culture, conforming to dominant norms and values while suppressing aspects of their Mexican identity.

The Struggle for Mexican American Identity

The dual cultural pressures experienced by Mexican Americans represent a deeply troubling aspect of their lived experience, casting a shadow of profound internal conflict and identity crisis. The weight of straddling two cultures, each with its expectations and norms, can be overwhelming, leading to a constant struggle to reconcile conflicting aspects of one's identity. This relentless battle often leaves Mexican Americans feeling adrift, torn between loyalty to their cultural heritage and the pressure to conform to mainstream American ideals. Not just that, the psychological toll of this perpetual balancing act cannot be overstated. The constant juggling of cultural identities can erode one's sense of self, creating feelings of alienation, self-doubt, and existential angst. The quest for belonging becomes an elusive pursuit as Mexican Americans grapple with the unsettling realization that they may never fully fit in anywhere.

In addition to the internal turmoil, Mexican Americans face external challenges stemming from their dual identity. Living between two cultures exposes them to a myriad of discriminatory attitudes, stereotypes, and microaggressions. They often face scrutiny, suspicion, and marginalization within their communities and broader society. These experiences of prejudice and exclusion further compound the already daunting challenges faced by Mexican American communities, deepening the wounds of intergenerational trauma and systemic injustice.

The ramifications of these dual cultural pressures are far-reaching and profound, permeating every aspect of Mexican American life. From education and employment to healthcare and social interactions, the discord between the two worlds is felt acutely, shaping the trajectory of individuals and communities alike. As we confront these sobering realities, we must acknowledge the depth of the struggle faced by Mexican Americans and work toward creating a more inclusive and equitable society. In such a society, all individuals can embrace their cultural heritages without fear or shame (Davis-Undiano, 2017).

Historical Injustices: Displacement & Enduring Discrimination

The legacy of historical injustices against marginalized communities, particularly Mexican Americans, continues to cast a long shadow over their lived experiences. From the violent displacement of Indigenous peoples to the discriminatory policies of the past, Mexican Americans have endured generations of systemic oppression and marginalization. For example, the forced relocation of Mexican Americans during the Mexican-American War and the subsequent Treaty of Guadalupe Hidalgo led to the loss of ancestral lands and communities, perpetuating cycles of poverty and disenfranchisement. Furthermore, discriminatory practices such as redlining, segregation, and the denial of civil rights have further entrenched inequalities and hindered socioeconomic mobility. These historical injustices have had long-term consequences, impacting the socioeconomic conditions of Mexican American communities while compounding inequities in education, healthcare, and employment.

Moreover, the enduring legacy of discrimination continues to manifest in contemporary society through racial profiling, unequal treatment under the law, and the perpetuation of harmful stereotypes. Addressing historical injustices requires reckoning with the past and confronting the systemic inequalities that persist in the present. It necessitates a commitment to truth, reconciliation, and reparative justice, including efforts to redress past harms and dismantle discriminatory structures. By acknowledging the historical roots of current inequities and working toward meaningful change, we can strive toward a more just and inclusive society for all. Therefore, the following sections contain examples of injustices against Mexican Americans.

The Zoot Suit Riots (1943)

The Zoot Suit Riots were a series of racially motivated attacks against Mexican American youths in Los Angeles, California, during World War II. White service members and civilians targeted Mexican American youths who wore zoot suits, which were considered flashy and extravagant. The riots escalated into violence as mobs of White attackers roamed the streets, assaulting and beating Mexican American youths. The riots reflected deep-seated racial tensions and discrimination against Mexican Americans, fueled by economic competition, wartime anxieties, and racial stereotypes perpetuated by the media.

The Sleepy Lagoon Murder Trial (1942)

The Sleepy Lagoon Murder Trial was a notorious case in which 22 Mexican American youths were wrongfully convicted of murder in Los Angeles. The trial centered around the death of a young man named José Díaz at a party near a reservoir known as the Sleepy Lagoon. The prosecution portrayed Mexican American youths as members of a "gang" and used racial stereotypes to secure convictions. The trial was marred by systemic racism, media sensationalism, and inadequate legal representation for the defendants. Despite widespread protests and appeals, the convictions were upheld, highlighting the systemic discrimination faced by Mexican Americans within the criminal justice system.

Operation Wetback (1954)

Operation Wetback was a government-initiated immigration crackdown launched in 1954, targeting Mexican immigrants living in the U.S. The operation, spearheaded by the Immigration and Naturalization Service, involved mass round-ups and deportations of Mexican immigrants, many of whom were legal residents or U.S. citizens. Human rights abuses, including the separation of families, detention in deplorable conditions, and deportations without due process, marked the operation. Operation Wetback reflected the government's discriminatory immigration policies and the pervasive anti-Mexican sentiment prevalent in American society during the 1950s.

Mendez v. Westminster (1947)

Mendez v. Westminster was a landmark legal case that challenged school segregation in California. In the 1940s, Mexican American children in California were often segregated into separate "Mexican schools," which provided inferior education compared to White schools. In 1945, Gonzalo and Felicitas Mendez filed a lawsuit on behalf of their children, arguing that school segregation based on race violated the 14th Amendment's equal protection clause. The case culminated in a federal court ruling in 1947, which declared school segregation unconstitutional in California. The ruling laid the groundwork for subsequent desegregation efforts nationwide and highlighted the fight for civil rights within Mexican American communities.

The Mexican Repatriation (1929–1936)

The Mexican Repatriation was a government-sponsored program during the Great Depression that forcibly deported hundreds of thousands of Mexican immigrants and Mexican Americans from the U.S. The repatriation, fueled by economic hardship and anti-immigrant sentiment, disproportionately targeted Mexican Americans, including U.S. citizens. Many Mexican Americans were coerced or deceived into leaving the country, resulting in the involuntary removal of entire families from their homes and communities. The repatriation exacerbated economic hardships and social upheaval within Mexican American communities, leading to long-lasting scars and intergenerational trauma.

Anguish & Reassessment of Identity Amid Racial Divides & Incorporating Anger Management Research

Amid enduring racial divides and systemic injustices, Mexican Americans grapple with profound anguish and a reassessment of their identity. The pervasive discrimination and marginalization they face prompt a deep existential questioning of their place in society and their sense of belonging. Mexican Americans often find themselves torn between the cultural heritage they cherish and the pressures to assimilate into a predominantly White mainstream culture. This internal conflict gives rise to feelings of alienation, self-doubt, and a search for authenticity in their identity.

Moreover, the racial divides within American society further exacerbate these struggles as Mexican Americans get the gist of complex intersections of race, ethnicity, and socioeconomic status. They confront racial stereotypes, microaggressions, and systemic barriers that hinder their social mobility and perpetuate cycles of inequality. This constant battle against discrimination and injustice takes a toll on their mental health and well-being, fueling a collective sense of anguish and frustration.

In response to these challenges, Mexican Americans engage in reassessment and reclamation of their identity. They seek to assert their cultural pride, reclaim their heritage, and challenge dominant narratives that marginalize their experiences. Through activism, community organizing, and cultural expression, they strive to create spaces of empowerment and solidarity where their voices are heard and their identities affirmed. As they confront the anguish of racial divides and reassess their identity in the face of systemic injustices, their determination to forge a more inclusive and equitable society serves as a beacon of hope and inspiration for future generations.

Incorporating Anger Management Research

In addressing the anguish and reassessment of identity amid racial divides experienced by Mexican Americans, integrating anger management research becomes imperative. The psychological toll of discrimination and marginalization often leads to feelings of anger, frustration, and helplessness within Mexican American communities. Anger management research offers valuable insights and strategies to deal with these complex emotions constructively. Mexican Americans can learn effective coping mechanisms and communication skills to express their emotions assertively and nondestructively by incorporating anger management research into interventions and support services. Techniques include mindfulness, cognitive restructuring, and conflict resolution, which empower individuals to address anger in a healthy and productive manner.

Furthermore, anger management research emphasizes the importance of identifying the underlying causes of anger, including societal injustices and systemic inequalities. By contextualizing anger within the broader social and historical context, Mexican Americans can validate their experiences and channel their anger toward collective action and advocacy for social change. Incorporating anger management research into educational curricula, community programs, and mental health services can also provide valuable resources and support for Mexican Americans facing the complexities of discrimination. Equipping them with the tools to manage their anger effectively will both empower them to assert their rights and dignity and help promote healing.

Addressing Anger Within Cultural Identity Struggles

Cultural identity struggles often evoke intense emotions, including anger, within Mexican American communities. The clash between preserving cultural heritage and assimilating into mainstream American society can fuel frustration, resentment, and anger. Addressing anger within cultural identity struggles requires a multifaceted approach that acknowledges the complexities of this experience.

Creating safe spaces for Mexican Americans to express and validate their emotions is essential. By initiating open dialogue and supportive environments, individuals can articulate their anger and explore its roots without fear of judgment or reprisal. Encouraging self-reflection and introspection helps individuals understand the underlying causes of their anger and empowers them to address these issues constructively. Promoting cultural pride and affirmation is pivotal in addressing anger within cultural identity struggles. Embracing and celebrating Mexican heritage fosters a sense of belonging and empowerment, counteracting feelings of alienation and disenfranchisement. Cultural education and immersion programs offer opportunities for Mexican Americans to reconnect with their roots and reclaim their identity with pride.

Immediate Actions to Alleviate Anguish in Cultural Identity Struggles

In addition to the urgency of providing access to mental health resources and support services, it is paramount to recognize the critical role they play in addressing the profound anguish and turmoil experienced within cultural identity struggles. Therapy, counseling, and support groups serve as indispensable lifelines, offering invaluable tools and coping mechanisms for managing the overwhelming anger and the intricate labyrinth of cultural identity. Moreover, culturally competent mental health care is imperative to ensure that individuals receive the compassionate and understanding support necessary to deal with their unique experiences and backgrounds with sensitivity.

The imperative for advocacy and activism cannot be overstated in confronting the systemic injustices that exacerbate cultural identity struggles and fuel the simmering anger within Mexican American communities. Through the collective mobilization for social change and relentless advocacy for policies that champion equity and inclusion, individuals can harness their anger toward catalyzing positive transformation. By rallying for systemic changes and amplifying their voices, individuals can challenge the entrenched structures of inequality and pave the way for a more just and inclusive society.

Addressing the deep-seated anger entrenched within cultural identity struggles necessitates a comprehensive and holistic approach. Such an approach must embrace emotional validation, cultural affirmation, access to mental health resources, and fervent advocacy for systemic change. By acknowledging and confronting the multifaceted layers of cultural identity, we can forge a more compassionate, empowering, and dignified environment where Mexican Americans can come into their identities gracefully.

Coping Mechanisms & Strategies for Managing Anger

In the face of cultural identity struggles and systemic injustices, individuals must acquire efficient coping mechanisms and tactics for anger management. These coping methods and tactics are excellent resources for managing the intricacies of rage in the context of cultural identity issues. One such method is mindfulness practice, which entails identifying one's thoughts, emotions, and physical sensations without judgment. Mindfulness can improve self-awareness and emotional control, allowing users to respond to anger triggers more clarity and serenity. Mindfulness practices, such as deep breathing exercises and body scans, allow people to examine their emotions without being overwhelmed, developing inner peace during hardship.

Additionally, cognitive-behavioral approaches can help challenge and reframe harmful thought patterns related to anger. Individuals can use cognitive restructuring to identify and confront illogical ideas or skewed thinking that feeds anger, replacing them with more balanced and realistic viewpoints. Individuals who learn to understand and question the underlying cognitive distortions that lead to anger can develop better ways of reading and responding to difficult situations, lowering the intensity and frequency of furious outbursts.

Furthermore, participating in healthy ways to express and release anger can be positive. This process may involve participating in physical activity, artistic expression, or writing to channel and release pent-up emotions healthily. Finding healthy outlets for anger enables people to process and express their feelings without engaging in harmful or destructive activities. Physical exercise, in particular, may be a valuable outlet for anger because it releases pent-up energy and stimulates the creation of endorphins, which are natural mood boosters. Receiving help from trustworthy friends, family members, or mental health experts may offer direction and affirmation in the face of anger. Building a support network of people who understand and sympathize with one's situation can provide comfort and perspective in times of difficulty. Furthermore, professional therapy or counseling may present individuals with the tools and strategies necessary to regulate anger effectively, as well as a secure environment to examine and process underlying feelings. Individuals who attend therapy might acquire insight into the underlying reasons for their anger, improve their coping skills, and discover healthy ways of expressing and controlling their emotions constructively.

Chapter 12

Decoding White Anger & Disparities – White Americans

Understanding White Anger

The term *White Americans* in this chapter refers to anyone of the White race who was born in America. This term can include descendants of the European continent. On the other hand, *White Americans* are also individuals born on the European continent who have received American citizenship. In contrast, *Europeans* are immigrants from the European continent who were not born in the U.S. and do not have American citizenship. This chapter will focus on White Americans, individuals of the White race born or with citizenship in the U.S.

White anger encompasses a complex array of emotions, including frustration, resentment, and fear, which are deeply rooted in perceptions of threat to White identity, status, or privilege. This anger often arises in response to perceived challenges to traditional power structures and social hierarchies, such as affirmative action policies or multiculturalism initiatives to promote diversity and inclusion. At its core, White anger reflects a sense of loss or erosion of perceived entitlements and advantages historically enjoyed by White Americans. As society evolves toward greater equality and diversity, some White individuals may feel threatened by the prospect of losing their perceived superiority and privilege. This threat to their social standing can evoke strong emotional reactions, leading to expressions of anger and resistance. White anger may also stem from a fear of change and uncertainty about the future.

As demographic shifts and cultural transformations redefine American society, some White individuals may feel disoriented and marginalized, leading to heightened feelings of insecurity and resentment. White anger is often fueled by narratives of victimization and perceived injustice, wherein White individuals perceive themselves as disadvantaged or marginalized in the face of initiatives aimed at promoting social justice and equity. This narrative of victimhood can exacerbate feelings of resentment and defiance as some White individuals resist efforts to address systemic inequalities and historical injustices.

Historical Context

Throughout American history, White anger has manifested prominently during periods of significant social upheaval, with perhaps no era more illustrative of this than the Civil Rights Movement of the 1960s. During this transformative period, efforts to dismantle institutionalized segregation and advance racial equality provoked a powerful backlash from segments of White society. The movement challenged deeply entrenched systems of racial hierarchy and discrimination, seeking to secure fundamental rights and liberties for Black Americans that had long been denied. As Black Americans and their allies mobilized through nonviolent protests, sit-ins, and marches to demand an end to segregation and racial injustice, they confronted fierce opposition from White supremacist groups, as well as from ordinary White citizens who felt threatened by the prospect of change.

For White Americans, particularly those in the South, where Jim Crow laws were deeply entrenched, the Civil Rights Movement represented a direct challenge to their social, economic, and political dominance. The prospect of desegregation and equal rights for Black Americans was perceived as a threat to their longstanding privileges and status as the dominant racial group. Consequently, this challenge to the existing social order sparked intense feelings of anger, resentment, and fear among some White Americans who viewed the movement as an assault on their ways of life. The backlash against the movement took various forms, ranging from violent resistance and intimidation tactics to more subtle forms of opposition, such as resistance to school integration and voting rights reforms. This resistance reflected a broader obstinance in the face of social change and a defense of White supremacy, fueled by deeply ingrained racial prejudices and anxieties about losing power and privilege.

Economic Discontent

Economic factors are pivotal in fomenting White anger, especially among working-class White Americans who perceive themselves as economically marginalized or displaced by the forces of globalization and technological progress. The erosion of traditional industries and outsourcing jobs to cheaper labor markets overseas have led to widespread job loss and wage stagnation in many communities. Consequently, working-class White Americans find themselves grappling with economic insecurity and diminished prospects for upward mobility. The decline of manufacturing and other blue-collar industries has profoundly impacted the economic well-being of many White Americans, particularly those in regions that were once industrial powerhouses. As factories shutter and jobs disappear, communities are left grappling with the social and economic fallout, including rising poverty rates, substance abuse, and declining infrastructure.

Moreover, the rise of automation and technological advancements has further exacerbated economic disparities, as many traditional jobs are rendered obsolete or require higher levels of skill and education. This issue leaves many working-class White Americans feeling left behind in an increasingly competitive and globalized economy, leading to feelings of resentment and frustration toward perceived elites and immigrants who are seen as benefiting from these changes.

Economic insecurity and downward mobility can also breed a sense of disillusionment with the American Dream, as many working-class White Americans struggle to make ends meet and provide for their families. This sense of economic precarity can fuel feelings of resentment toward perceived beneficiaries of social welfare programs. Frustration has also grown with political elites perceived as out of touch with the struggles of ordinary Americans.

Cultural Shifts

Changing cultural norms and demographic shifts have the potential to evoke strong emotions, including anger and nostalgia, among some White Americans who perceive their traditional values and way of life as under threat. Issues such as immigration, multiculturalism, and changing gender roles may be perceived as eroding White cultural identity and triggering defensive reactions. Immigration has long been a contentious issue in American society, and debates over immigration policy often center on questions of national identity and cultural assimilation. Some White Americans express concerns about the perceived dilution of American culture and values due to increased immigration, particularly from non-European countries. They may view immigrants as a threat to their ways of life and fear the loss of their cultural hegemony.

The promotion of multiculturalism and diversity initiatives is sometimes met with resistance from White Americans who perceive these efforts as prioritizing the interests of minority groups over their own. They may feel marginalized or excluded by initiatives promoting diversity and inclusion, leading to resentment and anger. Changing gender roles and norms around sexuality and family structure can also evoke strong reactions from some White Americans who adhere to traditional views of gender and family. For example, the increasing acceptance of LGBTQ+ rights may be perceived as a challenge to traditional notions of masculinity and femininity, leading to feelings of discomfort or anger.

Political Circumstances

The politicization of race and identity issues has significantly contributed to the worsening of White anger in American society. Politicians and media outlets frequently exploit racial anxieties and grievances to mobilize support among White voters, resulting in polarization and the amplification of White nationalist rhetoric. In recent years, the political circumstances in the U.S. have become increasingly polarized, with racial and identity issues playing a central role in shaping political discourse. Politicians on both sides of the aisle have sought to capitalize on White anxieties about demographic change, immigration, and cultural shifts to rally support and mobilize their base.

Some politicians and media outlets have adopted inflammatory rhetoric and fearmongering tactics to stoke White anger and resentment, framing issues such as immigration, affirmative action, and crime in racialized terms. This exploitation of racial anxieties serves to deepen divisions within society and perpetuate a sense of grievance among some White Americans who feel marginalized or disenfranchised. Moreover, the rise of White nationalist and far-right movements has further amplified White anger, providing a platform for extremist views and contributing to a climate of intolerance and hostility toward minority groups. Politicians who espouse xenophobic or racist ideologies often find support among segments of the White population who feel disillusioned with mainstream politics and perceive their interests as under threat.

Intersectionality

White anger intersects with various other social identities, including gender, class, and region, profoundly shaping individual experiences and perceptions. For instance, rural White Americans may feel disenfranchised and overlooked by urban elites, resulting in feelings of resentment and alienation. The intersectionality of White anger acknowledges that individuals' experiences of anger and frustration are influenced by multiple factors, including their gender, socioeconomic status, and geographic location. For instance, rural White Americans may feel marginalized by policies and narratives that prioritize urban areas, leading to a sense of neglect and frustration. In rural communities, economic opportunities may be limited, and access to essential services such as healthcare and education may be scarce. These issues can exacerbate feelings of economic insecurity and resentment toward perceived urban elites who are seen as benefiting from government resources and investment.

Furthermore, the gender dynamics within White communities can shape experiences of anger and resentment. Traditional gender roles may dictate expectations for men and women, leading to feelings of frustration and powerlessness when individuals perceive their roles and identities to be threatened or undermined. Regional differences play a significant role in shaping White anger. Rural areas with different values, priorities, and challenges may feel culturally distinct from urban centers. This issue can lead to a sense of cultural alienation and resentment toward policies and narratives that are perceived to prioritize urban interests over rural ones.

Exploring Anger & Thuggish Behavior

For years, concern has grown over the intersection of anger and thuggish behavior, particularly among specific segments of White American society. This phenomenon represents a significant public health crisis, with implications for individual well-being and societal harmony. Anger, when left unchecked and unmanaged, can manifest in various forms of aggressive or antisocial behavior, commonly referred to as *thuggish behavior*. This behavior encompasses a range of actions, including verbal aggression, physical violence, and intimidation tactics, often directed toward marginalized or vulnerable populations.

Historical Examples of Thuggish Behavior

The following sections contain examples of thuggish behavior.

Charlottesville, Virginia, 2017

The "Unite the Right" rally in Charlottesville, Virginia, in 2017, organized by White nationalists, led to violence. James Alex Fields, Jr., a participant, drove into counter-protesters, killing Heather Heyer and injuring others. The event underscored racial tensions and the rise of far-right extremism in America, sparking national outrage and renewed discussions about hate groups and systemic racism. Fields was convicted of first-degree murder and sentenced to life in prison. However, the tragedy served as a poignant reminder of the urgent need to confront bigotry and promote inclusivity in society.

Emmett Till Lynching, 1955

In 1955, Emmett Till, a 14-year-old African American boy, was brutally murdered in Mississippi for reportedly flirting with a White woman. His killers, Roy Bryant and J. W. Milam, were acquitted by an all-White jury, exposing the deep-seated racism of the Jim Crow South. Till's lynching galvanized the Civil Rights Movement, serving as a catalyst for change and igniting national outrage. The injustice of his death and the lack of accountability for his murderers underscored the pervasive racial violence and discrimination endured by Black Americans during that era.

Tulsa Race Massacre, 1921

In 1921, Tulsa, Oklahoma, witnessed one of the most brutal acts of racial violence in American history. A White mob attacked the prosperous African American neighborhood of Greenwood, known as "Black Wall Street". The violence resulted in the deaths of hundreds of Black residents and the destruction of numerous businesses and homes. This horrific event, known as the Tulsa Race Massacre, highlighted the systemic racism and anti-Black sentiment prevalent in the U.S. at the time. The massacre also underscored the strength of the Black community in the face of extreme difficulties and the urgent need for racial justice and reconciliation.

Murder of Vincent Chin, 1982

In 1982, Vincent Chin, a Chinese American man, was brutally beaten to death by two White men, Ronald Ebens and Michael Nitz, in Detroit, Michigan. The attack stemmed from anti-Asian sentiment amid rising tensions in the auto industry. Despite public outcry, the perpetrators received lenient sentences, underscoring racial injustice in the legal system. The murder of Vincent Chin brought attention to hate crimes against Asian Americans and sparked a national conversation about racism and the need for stronger protections for marginalized communities.

What Fuels Anger & Thuggish Behavior Among White Americans?

The prevalence of anger and thuggish behavior among specific segments of White American society reflects deeper societal issues, including systemic racism, economic inequality, and cultural dislocation. Individuals who feel disenfranchised or marginalized may channel their anger into acts of aggression to assert power or reclaim control in their lives. Moreover, the normalization and glorification of aggression in media and popular culture further perpetuate this cycle of violence and hostility. From reality television shows to online forums, aggressive behavior is often celebrated and rewarded, reinforcing harmful stereotypes and promoting a culture of violence.

How Can We Address It?

Addressing the public health crisis of anger and thuggish behavior requires an approach that is not only comprehensive but can also address the root cause while promoting prevention and intervention strategies. This process includes investing in mental health resources and support services, implementing community-based interventions to address underlying social determinants of aggression, and promoting nonviolent conflict resolution and anger management skills. Prioritizing prevention and systemic change can help create safer, more peaceful communities for everyone in America.

Addressing Anger Toward Other Races

In addressing anger by White Americans toward other races, several pivotal strategies are essential for a more inclusive and equitable society. First, it is imperative to acknowledge and actively challenge implicit biases and ingrained prejudices. By promoting self-reflection and education, individuals can become more aware of their biases and work toward dismantling them.

Second, cultivating empathy and understanding through exposure to diverse perspectives is essential for providing empathy and compassion toward individuals from marginalized communities. Encouraging cross-cultural education in educational institutions and workplaces is crucial for promoting mutual respect and appreciation for diversity. Addressing systemic injustices through advocacy for social justice reforms is vital in addressing the root causes of racial tensions. This need involves advocating for policies, educating their children and family members, and implementing initiatives within their communities to dismantle institutionalized racism and promote equality for all.

Third, initiating constructive dialogue by creating safe spaces and facilitated discussions allows for meaningful engagement and collective problem-solving. In this way, platforms can be provided for open and honest conversations. Communities can work toward building bridges and addressing the underlying issues contributing to anger and hostility toward other races.

Instances of Anger Toward Other Races Leading to Dire Situations

Charleston Church Shooting, 2015

The Charleston Church Shooting in 2015 stands as a harrowing example of the dire consequences of anger and hatred toward other races. Dylann Roof, a young White supremacist, meticulously planned and executed a brutal attack on the historic Emanuel African Methodist Episcopal Church in Charleston, South Carolina. On the evening of June 17, 2015, Roof entered the church during a Bible study session attended by African American parishioners, including the esteemed pastor, Reverend Clementa Pinckney. Roof sat with the group for approximately an hour before he suddenly opened fire, unleashing a barrage of bullets upon the unsuspecting worshippers. In the ensuing chaos, nine innocent African American churchgoers tragically lost their lives, including Reverend Pinckney. The victims ranged in age from 26 to 87 years old, and their senseless deaths sent shockwaves of grief and outrage across the nation.

Roof's heinous act was motivated by his virulent White supremacist beliefs and fueled by a deeply ingrained hatred toward African Americans. Before the shooting, Roof had espoused racist ideologies and expressed his desire to incite a race war. The chilling manifesto, which he published online before the attack, revealed his warped worldview and his intention to perpetrate acts of violence against Black individuals.

Atlanta Spa Shootings, 2021

The Atlanta Spa Shootings of 2021 epitomizes the tragic consequences of anger directed toward individuals of other races. In a series of targeted attacks, a White gunman embarked on a spree that targeted three Asian-owned spas in the Atlanta area. The rampage resulted in the deaths of eight people, most of whom were women of Asian descent. The victims, innocent employees, and patrons going about their daily lives fell victim to senseless violence fueled by racism and misogyny.

The shootings sent shockwaves through Asian American communities nationwide, reigniting fears of racially motivated attacks. This moment highlights the intersection of racism and sexism faced by Asian women. The perpetrator's actions, driven by a toxic combination of racial hatred and objectification, underscored the urgent need to address the escalating anti-Asian sentiment and hate crimes sweeping the country.

El Paso Walmart Shooting, 2019

The El Paso Walmart Shooting of 2019 is a stark reminder of the devastating impact of anger directed toward individuals of different races. In this horrific attack, a White supremacist specifically targeted Hispanic shoppers at a Walmart in El Paso, Texas. Armed with a high-powered rifle, the gunman indiscriminately opened fire, resulting in the deaths of 23 innocent people and causing numerous others to sustain severe injuries.

The massacre shocked the Hispanic community and the nation as a whole, laying bare the deadly consequences of xenophobia and racial hatred. The perpetrator's heinous actions were motivated by a virulent ideology of White supremacy, which scapegoated immigrants and fueled anti-Latino sentiment. The attack was a brutal manifestation of the deep-seated racism and bigotry that continue to plague society.

Murder of Ahmaud Arbery, 2020

The murder of Ahmaud Arbery in 2020 serves as a tragic example of the deadly consequences of racial hatred and aggression toward individuals of other races. Ahmaud Arbery, an African American man, was simply jogging through a residential neighborhood in Glynn County, Georgia, when he was pursued and fatally shot by three White men. The attackers, armed and fueled by racist assumptions, targeted Ahmaud solely because of his race.

The brutal killing of Ahmaud Arbery sparked national outrage and reignited conversations about systemic racism and injustice in the U.S. It underscores the pervasive dangers faced by Black individuals simply going about their daily lives. The attack highlights the need for meaningful change in law enforcement practices and accountability.

Impact of Recent Events: Capitol Attack

The Capitol Attack on January 6, 2021, reverberated across the nation, leaving a profound impact on American society. The violent insurrection, perpetrated by a predominantly White mob, sought to overturn the results of the 2020 presidential election and disrupt the democratic process. The shocking scenes of chaos and destruction unfolded as rioters breached the Capitol building, resulting in multiple deaths, injuries, and widespread damage.

The Capitol Attack shed light on the dangers of unchecked anger and extremism within specific segments of White American society. It exposed the deep-rooted divisions, radicalization, and misinformation that have increased in recent years, fueled by political polarization and inflammatory rhetoric. The brazen display of White supremacy and anti-government sentiment underscores the urgent need to confront the rising tide of domestic terrorism and hate groups.

Moreover, the Capitol Attack further eroded public trust in democratic institutions and underscored the fragility of America's democratic norms. It prompted soul-searching and introspection about the state of democracy and the challenges facing the nation in an increasingly polarized and volatile political climate. In the aftermath of the Capitol Attack, there have been calls for accountability, justice, and reconciliation. The event served as a wake-up call for law enforcement agencies, policymakers, and society as a whole to confront the root causes of extremism and address the systemic failures that allowed such an attack to occur. It also galvanized efforts to strengthen democratic institutions, safeguard civil liberties, and promote unity and healing in a deeply divided nation.

Shifting Perspectives for Positive Change Toward Anger

In confronting the pervasive issue of anger and thuggish behavior among White Americans, urgent attention must be paid to adopting innovative and unconventional strategies that challenge the status quo. We must delve beyond the conventional methods and into realms of creativity and empathy to address this pressing concern. Harnessing the power of art and creative expression, mindfulness and meditation practices, community building, and mutual aid initiatives are paramount. Additionally, using humor and satire, along with peer support and mentorship programs, can offer critical avenues for introspection and growth. Moreover, embracing outdoor and adventure therapy can provide a unique opportunity for individuals to confront their emotions and cultivate determination.

Only by embracing these unconventional approaches can we hope to foster genuine empathy, self-awareness, and constructive dialogue within White American communities, ultimately paving the way for positive change and reducing aggression. The urgency of this endeavor cannot be overstated, as the consequences of inaction continue to reverberate throughout U.S. society, perpetuating harm and division. However, as explored in the following sections, some approaches can be quite effective in the long run.

Art & Creative Expression

White Americans may use art and creative expression as tools for introspection and social change. They should be encouraged to explore their emotions and experiences through painting, poetry, music, and storytelling. Art can be a powerful catalyst for empathy, self-awareness, and dialogue. People may form a deeper understanding of the impact of anger and aggression on individuals and communities.

Mindfulness & Meditation

Mindfulness and meditation practices should be promoted to cultivate emotional regulation and self-awareness. Workshops and training programs should be offered to teach White Americans how to manage stress, anxiety, and anger through mindfulness techniques. By incorporating mindfulness into daily life, individuals can develop a greater understanding and more effective approaches to resolving conflict.

Community Building & Mutual Aid

Leaders should facilitate community-building initiatives that foster solidarity and mutual support among diverse groups. White Americans should be encouraged to participate in grassroots organizing, mutual aid networks, and community-led initiatives aimed at addressing systemic issues, such as poverty, inequality, and racism.

Humor & Satire

People can harness the power of humor and satire to challenge stereotypes, deflate tension, and promote critical thinking. White Americans should be encouraged to engage in satire and comedy that highlight the absurdity of racism, bigotry, and aggression.

Peer Support & Mentorship

Leaders should establish peer support networks and mentorship programs that provide guidance, encouragement, and accountability for individuals struggling with anger and aggression. White Americans should be paired with mentors from diverse backgrounds. They can offer perspective, empathy, and guidance on intergroup dynamics while addressing bias and prejudice.

Outdoor & Adventure Therapy

People can explore the therapeutic benefits of outdoor and adventure activities to promote personal growth and healing. Wilderness therapy programs and outdoor experiential learning opportunities should be offered to challenge individuals to build and develop interpersonal skills outside their comfort zones. Embracing these innovative approaches and thinking outside the box can result in new pathways being taken toward positive change in White Americans regarding their anger and thuggish behavior.

These strategies emphasize creativity, connection, and self-reflection, helping individuals transform their attitudes and behaviors in meaningful ways. Such strategies may mitigate the health disparities discussed in the following section.

Health Disparities That Impact White Americans

Health disparities are the difference between a given group of people in America in attaining full health potential that can be determined or estimated by differences in occurrence, mortality, burden of the illness, and other harmful health conditions. As mentioned in a previous chapter, White Americans generally experience better healthcare outcomes compared to other racial and ethnic groups in the U.S.; however, they still suffer from other health disparities more, compared to other groups in the country. These health disparities include mental health issues and issues from health treatments that include opioid addiction and overdose, skin cancer, colorectal cancer, suicide, prostate cancer, breast cancer, osteoporosis/fractures, cystic fibrosis, alcoholism, and more.

Mental Health

An example of health disparities among this population is mental health-related issues. For instance, U.S. White Americans have higher rates of suicide compared to other racial and ethnic populations. In 2020 alone, 69% of American deaths due to suicide were White males (KSHB News, 2022). Although this issue is the leading cause of mortality among American citizens in the country, with 11 suicide mortalities per 100,000 people being White, people aged 65 and above commit suicide at almost three times the average rate (Yin, 2018).

Opioid addiction and overdoses also show disparities between White Americans and other racial and ethnic groups. This issue is considered the most prominent health disparity, leading to mortality among this population. The main contributing factor includes high rates of self-prescription of opioids within White communities. Opioid overdose-related deaths in the U.S. initially increased most intensely among White Americans, particularly non-Hispanic White men in their mid-40s to late 50s. According to the Centers for Disease Control and Prevention (2022), this incidence is primarily due to the overprescription of pain medications.

Health Issues

Rural White populations in the U.S. tend to be disproportionately disadvantaged by various health issues, with primary health issues being heart disease, stroke, and cancer. Rural populations also tend to have higher rates of mental health problems and substance abuse than urban populations. The suicide rate among rural populations is 1.5 times higher than in urban populations. (Ivey-Stephenson et al., 2017). Two main reasons behind these disparities are poor access to health care and lack of access to skilled healthcare providers in rural areas (Seigel, 2019). Many rural hospitals are at risk of closing, leaving hundreds, if not thousands, of White people without access to reliable healthcare. Rural counties tend to have fewer psychologists and psychiatrists, leaving many people suffering from mental health problems unable to seek help (Centers for Disease Control and Prevention, 2024).

Skin cancer is characterized by two types: melanoma and nonmelanoma. There are 5,000,000 new cases identified in the U.S. alone. The three most diagnosed types of skin cancer in the country are melanoma, squamous cell carcinoma, and basal cell carcinoma. The U.S. government spent, on average, US$8.1 billion for skin cancer treatment between 2007 and 2011, with an average death toll of 600,000 yearly (Aggarwal et al., 2021). Other types of cancer, such as colorectal cancer, have become increasingly more common among younger White populations and experienced an increase in cases among those younger than 55 years to 20% in 2019, a jump from 11% in 1995 (Siegel et al., 2023). Prostate cancer represented the most common type of cancer among White men in the U.S., with approximately 248,000 new cases being diagnosed in 2021 (Siegel et al., 2023). Breast cancer was only the second most common cause of cancer deaths among White American women, with mortality the highest among women aged 65 (Ellington et al., 2023).

Cystic fibrosis is one of the most life-shortening genetic disorders among the White population. It is the second most common disorder in the U.S., with one in 3,500 being affected since birth (Oates et al., 2021). Patients' care and treatment patterns differ based on their access to public health resources and socioeconomic status. On the other hand, osteoporosis is one of the leading causes of death among older White adults in the U.S., particularly White women. On average, White Hispanic women were 34% less likely to undergo additional screening and testing for osteoporosis than White American women (Ruiz-Esteves et al., 2022). Alcoholism was found to be more common among White American men than White women (68% compared to 64%, respectively). White males were likely to consume three times as much as women in alcohol per year, more likely to receive treatment in a hospital for alcohol-related injury or disease, and more likely die from alcohol-related causes (White, 2020).

White Americans are encouraged to focus on improving their population disparities because their efforts can promote equity, justice, and social change. It can help raise awareness, promote accountability, challenge privilege, inspire action, and build solidarity across diverse communities. In addition, public platforms should start holding White Americans accountable for their disparities to foster a more comprehensive, empathic, and effective approach to addressing social inequalities. This balanced focus can help create more equitable solutions that benefit all communities and promote a deeper understanding of the multifaceted nature of inequality. It can help raise awareness within this population and hold White Americans accountable for their disparities instead of constantly publicizing the challenges of other racial groups for several reasons. These reasons include understanding inequality, promoting self-reflection and responsibility, encouraging inclusive possible solutions, challenging stereotypes and simplistic narratives, building empathy and solidarity, highlighting intersectionality, advancing equity for all, and preventing neglect of specific issues.

Chapter 13
Building Bridges & Fostering Understanding

Harnessing Empathy Across Cultures

Building bridges begins with empathy—a strong desire to understand the lives and perspectives of others, as proven in earlier chapters. People of varied backgrounds have unique problems and concerns determined by societal dynamics and historical imbalances. Individuals can transcend cultural barriers by adopting empathy as a guiding principle and cultivating genuine connections based on compassion and mutual respect. Communities can better understand the human condition by immersing themselves in the stories and feelings of others, building bonds that surpass superficial differences, and providing a sense of shared humanity. Empathy builds bridges between individuals, communities, cultures, and generations, establishing a more inclusive and peaceful society where empathy is the foundation of collective growth and understanding.

Dialogue as a Transformative Force

Dialogue effectively bridges gaps and fosters comprehension. Individuals may challenge prejudices, demolish biases, and find common ground during variety by engaging in honest and real talk. Communities may foster empathy, strengthen trust, and build a communal sense of shared humanity to cross-cultural and ideological boundaries by creating venues for debates and exchanges. Through cultivating respectful participation and genuine contact, society can gracefully manage the complexities of diversity, creating understanding and paving the path for forgiveness and mutual respect. Empathy begins in the fertile ground of debate, while bonds of togetherness form and weave a harmonious togetherness and ideas that enrich the fabric of society.

Seeking Common Ground Amidst Diversity

Building bridges involves a steadfast commitment to discovering common ground within the diversity of humanity. Despite the disparities and tensions revealed in earlier discussions, a core unity underpins our existence, grounded in shared values and aspirations. Cultivating connections that transcend surface disparities and focus on mutual understanding and empathy enables individuals to bridge divides. Individuals can forge connections that transcend cultural and societal boundaries by shifting focus toward shared goals and aspirations. Viewing situations through the lens of commonality dissolves barriers and constructs bridges, nurturing a collective spirit of inclusivity and collaboration. In the quest for unity amidst diversity, people embark on a journey of exploration, unraveling the ties that unite us as members of the human race.

Education & Cultural Exchange

Exposure to other ideas and experiences is essential for developing understanding and empathy. As previously said, people can use cultural exchange programs, educational efforts, and intergroup conversation forums to engage in mutual learning, challenge prejudices, and broaden their perspectives. People who value cultural diversity and acknowledge human experience may acquire greater empathy and appreciation for the world's complexities. Individuals gain insights into the complexities of human life by exploring numerous narratives and lived experiences, which leads to a better understanding of the interconnectedness of our shared humanity.

Putting Theory Into Practice

Opportunities for bridge-building can span a spectrum, from local grassroots initiatives to global cross-cultural alliances. Based on the narratives and experiences shared earlier, individuals are motivated to take concrete steps toward building understanding and connection within their communities. They play a pivotal role in nurturing a more compassionate, equitable, and interconnected society by actively listening, engaging in meaningful dialogue, and advocating for empathy and inclusion. By amplifying diverse voices and perspectives, barriers are dismantled, empathy is cultivated, and a culture of mutual respect and understanding is nurtured. Recognizing the transformative potential of bridge-building endeavors, communities can catalyze positive change and establish inclusive spaces where every segment of society feels valued, heard, and empowered to contribute to the collective well-being.

Intersections of Anger, Resilience, & Advocacy

The Fire of Anger

Beneath the facade of societal harmony lies a simmering cauldron of anger, an enduring flame fueled by the deep-seated injustices inflicted upon communities of color throughout the annals of history. This anger is not merely a passing sentiment; it is also a righteous indignation born from centuries of disenfranchisement, discrimination, and violence. From the indelible scars left by the brutal institution of slavery to the continuous onslaught of racial profiling and police brutality, the embers of anger burn brightly, refusing to be quenched. This fury, embedded in the collective consciousness of the oppressed, acts as a catalyst for change. This powerful force drives individuals and communities alike to rise, resist, and demand responsibility. It is a visceral reaction to the ingrained inequities that pervade every stratum of society, from stark discrepancies in access to decent education and career prospects to widespread injustices in healthcare and the criminal justice system.

When confronted with systemic oppression and structural violence, the rage of oppressed groups becomes a rallying cry for justice and equality. Their rage sparks the flames of activism, pushing people to join the chorus of dissent, challenge the current quo, and chart a course for a more equitable future. Meaningful change begins to take root via the transforming power of this collective fury as communities band together in solidarity to deconstruct the oppressive structures that have long kept them excluded and disadvantaged.

The Dedication of Spirit

Amidst turmoil and despair, a light of tremendous perseverance shines brilliantly, illuminating the road ahead with its determination to endure and conquer. This attitude of power serves as the foundation for communities of color, demonstrating the human soul's unbreakable tenacity and courage. Despite the heavy weight of tyranny and suffering, disadvantaged people have demonstrated an astonishing capacity to adapt, survive, and thrive. From the hallowed grounds of the Civil Rights Movement, where echoes of freedom and justice reverberate through history, to the resounding chants of the Black Lives Matter movement echoing in the streets today, the courage of marginalized communities is a testament to the power of the human spirit to overcome seemingly insurmountable odds.

In the face of systematic injustice and institutionalized racism, endurance becomes a powerful force for change, enabling people and communities to reclaim their agency and humanity. Endurance is a fortitude formed during problems, tempered by the flames of struggle and sacrifice, and filled with a drive to carve out a future marked by justice, equality, and dignity for all. As oppressed populations negotiate the dangerous terrain of America's racial condition, their tenacity acts as a beacon of hope, lighting the path forward and motivating future generations to stand tall during injustice. Through unshakeable spirit and endurance, communities discover the strength to persist, resist, and ultimately triumph over the forces seeking to diminish their humanity and deny their worth.

The Call to Advocacy

The symphony of struggle, rage, and power combine to create a powerful call to advocacy—a clarion call that echoes across disadvantaged communities, demanding justice, equality, and structural reform. It is a call to collective action that inspires people to rise above despair, raise their voices in unity, and pave a path to a better tomorrow. Advocacy may take several forms, ranging from grassroots organization to political action challenging the established quo. It is intertwined into the fabric of legal fights fought in courtrooms and the painstaking efforts of community outreach initiatives dedicated to lifting the most vulnerable among us. At its foundation, advocacy is motivated by a strong sense of urgency and determination to dismantle the repressive systems perpetuating inequality and injustice.

As underrepresented communities band together to create a more just and equitable society, advocacy shines as a beacon of hope in the darkness. It guides the path forward with unrelenting determination and dedication to change. The transforming force of advocacy amplifies the voices of the oppressed, elevates their experiences, and makes their demands for justice and equality heard. Advocacy-inspired collective action sows the seeds of change, which are planted in the fertile soil of resistance and grow into a future where everyone is valued, respected, and free to live their lives with dignity and purpose.

Journeys of Emotional Turmoil & Courage in Marginalized Communities

The Intersection of Mental Health & Racial Trauma

Marginalized populations are embedded in the fabric of institutional oppression and racial injustice, laden with both overt displays of prejudice and internal mental health conflicts. Racial trauma, a ubiquitous result of systematic racism, causes profound scars in the mind, throwing people into despair and anguish. The constant bombardment of microaggressions, structural violence, and intergenerational trauma creates a cycle of psychological agony that pervades oppressed communities' collective awareness.

Despite the turbulence, a tribute to the human spirit's tenacity emerges. These groups tap into a reservoir of inner strength and courage, establishing paths to healing and restoration. Individuals regain control over their mental health by cultivating coping strategies, community support networks, and cultural practices, traversing the turbulent terrain of racial trauma with bravery as guiding beacons.

The Burden of Racial Trauma

Racial trauma causes significant scars in the psyche, locking people in a maze of mental health issues. Anxiety and despair throw smothering shadows, and the creeping phantom of PTSD lurks in the depths of the psyche. The weight of racial trauma rests heavily on the shoulders of individuals who endure its burdens, leaving them with a slew of psychiatric problems. Every day, the assault of microaggressions, institutional racism, and intergenerational trauma inflicts new scars, continuing a never-ending cycle of psychological suffering. This unremitting onslaught erodes the fundamental fabric of mental well-being, putting people on the verge of despair. The toll is tremendous, as the unseen wounds of racial trauma cut deep furrows in the mentality, leaving a legacy of misery and suffering.

Despite the gloom, glimmers of power emerge as people muster the courage to face their demons and establish a road to healing. Recognizing the significant impact of racial trauma on mental health allows us to begin to demolish the oppressive structures that perpetuate this cycle of suffering. We can build a future where all people can thrive emotionally and mentally.

Cultivating Strength During Hardships

Individuals from disadvantaged groups demonstrate incredible strength as they manage the intricacies of their mental health journeys despite the significant barriers inflicted by racial trauma. These individuals create routes to healing and restoration by drawing on cultural strengths, social support networks, and ancestral wisdom. They are rooted in the traditions and beliefs passed down through generations and use their strength to face hardship. They create strength via self-care routines, prioritizing their emotional well-being and engaging in spiritually nourishing activities. Whether via mindfulness techniques, artistic expression, or reconnecting with cultural traditions, self-care provides pillars of strength during chaos.

Equally important are the relationships of community support that help people on their road to healing. Within oppressed groups, networks of solidarity and mutual assistance serve as a lifeline of support, providing empathy, understanding, and validation to people dealing with the repercussions of racial trauma. Furthermore, collective resistance is an effective method for reclaiming control over mental health and enacting systemic change. By organizing, agitating, and mobilizing for social justice, disadvantaged groups address the core causes of racial trauma, aiming toward a future in which all people may exist free of oppression.

Christopher A. Lowery, DHSc, CLCP

The Imperative for Culturally Competent Mental Health Advocacy

Immediate action is needed to build culturally competent mental health advocacy and support programs while addressing the interconnected issues of racial trauma and mental health. This critical part emphasizes the need to provide accessible and affirming mental health treatment that recognizes and addresses underrepresented populations' unique experiences and needs. By prioritizing culturally responsive methods of therapy, advocacy, and policy reform, stakeholders may lead efforts to deconstruct structural barriers to mental health equality and create pathways to recovery in racial trauma-affected communities. Recognizing the different cultural origins and life experiences of those seeking mental health care is critical to this effort. Culturally competent mental health services are attentive to the cultural subtleties and traditions of varied groups, and they actively collaborate with community members to cocreate solutions that reflect their unique viewpoints and beliefs.

Furthermore, advocacy efforts must focus on addressing the underlying inequities and injustices that sustain mental health disparities in underrepresented populations. This process includes pushing for laws and activities that emphasize equitable access to mental health resources, address social determinants of mental health, and encourage antiracist practices in mental health facilities. In addition to offering direct services, mental health advocacy should encourage collaboration and partnership with community-based groups, grassroots movements, and cultural institutions.

Public Health Approaches for Addressing Anger Crisis

Anger is sometimes disregarded in the field of mental health even though it has a profound influence on communities, altering social dynamics and individual well-being. This subpoint discusses the need for public health techniques to address the widespread rage issue, arguing for systemic interventions prioritizing prevention, education, and community-based solutions. At its root, public health acknowledges that anger is a social issue with far-reaching consequences. Public health programs address the core causes of anger and its repercussions at the population level by moving the focus from individual illness to communal well-being.

Prevention emerges as a critical component of public health approaches to anger management, stressing early intervention and proactive steps to reduce the risk factors that lead to anger and violence. This process requires implementing policies and initiatives promoting social fairness, economic stability, and access to excellent education and healthcare while addressing the root causes of anger and violence. Education is also essential in public health measures; it raises awareness and fosters knowledge of anger as a normal and natural emotion with appropriate manifestations. Individuals can better negotiate anger constructively and nonviolently when emotional intelligence, conflict resolution skills, and empathy-building activities are promoted in schools, workplaces, and community contexts.

Furthermore, community-based treatments are critical components of public health approaches to anger management, using the power of social networks and grassroots activity to promote collective healing. These treatments range from peer support groups and therapeutic justice projects to trauma-informed care and community policing reforms. Such treatments enable communities to deal with anger and conflict in culturally appropriate, inclusive, and powerful ways.

Public health methods provide a comprehensive framework for dealing with the rage problem while acknowledging the interdependence of individual well-being, social justice, and unity among the community. These techniques prioritize prevention, education, and community participation. Such techniques can change social attitudes regarding anger while creating favorable conditions for healing, reconciliation, and peace.

Promoting Understanding, Acceptance, & Unity

Cultivating Empathy

Recognizing the Importance of Empathy

Recognizing empathy as a fundamental component in developing understanding and acceptance is critical in diverse societies. Empathy allows people to connect profoundly with others, overcoming differences and cultivating a feeling of shared humanity. Communities may bridge differences, create trust, and promote inclusion by empathizing with people from different backgrounds and experiences. Empathy is a guiding principle in this approach, promoting meaningful interactions and cultivating surroundings that foster mutual respect and acceptance.

Cultivating Empathy in Communities

Implementing comprehensive educational programs and activities is critical for cultivating empathy in various contexts, including schools, workplaces, and local communities. These programs should include various activities such as workshops, training, and interactive exercises to improve empathy skills and cultivate a culture of understanding and compassion. Individuals may gain empathy for the experiences and views of others by incorporating empathy-building strategies into school curricula, workplace training programs, and community outreach efforts. This proactive strategy creates the groundwork for building inclusive settings where empathy develops, resulting in healthy social interactions and relationships.

Nurturing Environments of Compassion

Creating inclusive workplaces is critical, as it allows people to overcome personal prejudices, make genuine relationships, and foster empathy via active listening and perspective-taking. These places promote a culture of openness and understanding, allowing people to sympathize with other points of view and experiences. Active listening and perspective-taking help people develop the ability to empathize with the feelings and perspectives of others, encouraging stronger relationships and mutual respect. Empathy becomes a guiding principle in such settings by building social relationships and instilling a sense of belonging and togetherness among all community members.

Facilitating Dialogue

Creating Platforms for Dialogue

Formal venues, such as neighborhood town halls or online discussion groups, are critical for open and polite conversation across varied perspectives and backgrounds. These forums enable individuals to engage in productive discourse, share viewpoints, and exchange ideas courteously and inclusively. By outlining norms for polite communication and regulation, these forums guarantee that all views are heard and respected, building a culture of mutual understanding and cooperation. Communities may use these organized talks to overcome gaps, create trust, and collaborate on common goals while encouraging unity and collective action.

Exchanging Perspectives

Encouraging people to share their unique experiences is critical for creating an environment where active listening and empathic examination of opposing ideas lead to mutual understanding. Individuals are empowered to engage in meaningful discourse and create empathy for the experiences of others by establishing environments that recognize and respect varied opinions. Active listening demonstrates a sincere desire to learn and sympathize with opposing ideas, building connections based on mutual respect and empathy. This culture of open-mindedness and sensitivity fosters positive talks, which should increase understanding and promote community harmony.

Building Bridges of Understanding

Dialogue is vital for establishing a sense of togetherness and solidarity among groups with diverse cultural, ethnic, or ideological roots. Communities may participate in productive talks that transcend divides and develop bridges of empathy and understanding by fostering respectful and open communication opportunities. Individuals may use dialogue to express their viewpoints, challenge prejudices, and develop empathy for one another's experiences. This collaborative method promotes unity and solidarity, allowing communities to achieve similar goals and overcome common obstacles.

Mobilizing for Collective Action

Committing to Justice & Equity

People and communities must unite around shared justice, fairness, and inclusion principles to confront structural concerns and promote social change. Communities may mobilize collective action to combat entrenched injustices and push for fundamental reforms by uniting around shared values. Individuals may use grassroots organizing, advocacy campaigns, and community-led initiatives to effect good change and build a more fair and inclusive society. Communities may use their collective strength to break down structural obstacles, elevate disadvantaged voices, and promote social justice agendas by cultivating a feeling of solidarity and shared purpose.

Grassroots Organizing

Empowering local communities to organize and mobilize for collective action through grassroots movements, advocacy campaigns, and community projects is critical for achieving significant social progress. Communities may organize their members to fight for policy reforms, raise awareness about important issues, and hold institutions responsible for dealing with systemic injustices by offering resources, training, and support. Communities may use grassroots organizing to amplify their voices, form alliances, and impact change from the bottom up. Communities can make a long-term difference and create a more just and equitable society by cultivating a culture of civic involvement and collective empowerment.

Amplifying Marginalized Voices

Centering the voices and experiences of underrepresented populations is critical in collaborative efforts to break down institutional obstacles, highlight various viewpoints, and promote social justice goals. Communities may guarantee that their concerns and experiences are heard and addressed by emphasizing the voices of those most impacted by injustice. This process entails developing venues for marginalized people to communicate their stories, viewpoints, and skills while actively including them in decision-making. By focusing on disadvantaged voices, communities may collaborate to produce more inclusive and effective systemic solutions than before, eventually leading to greater equality and justice for all parts of society.

Chapter 14
Conclusion

This self-help book delved deeply into the varied fabric of the American experience, connecting a diverse range of experiences and topics. It explored the core of the American Dream, traversing the maze of societal obstacles that follow its pursuit. It revealed the many layers of the National Crisis and Cause for Change, systemic inequities, and cultural identity problems that have pervaded the quest for achievement and belonging via the varied viewpoints of various cultures. By peeking through the kaleidoscope of human experiences, the book illuminated the difficulties of pursuing the illusive American Dream, showing the dreams, concerns, and goals that motivate people from all walks of life. The book explored American life from the corridors of power to the edges of society, illustrating the shared struggles and divergent realities that have defined the country's collective consciousness. Each chapter took readers on a journey of introspection and empathy, forcing them to confront the underlying inconsistencies and complexity of the American Dream. The book's sophisticated examination aimed to spark conversation, encourage advocacy, and empower people to combat injustice and create a more equal future for future generations.

Within the maze of issues covered, the book emphasized the critical roles of empathy, conversation, and collective action as necessary instruments for combating injustice and cultivating mutual understanding. It acted as a rallying cry for advocacy campaigns that aggressively remove repressive systems while elevating the voices of underrepresented populations. The book encouraged readers to engage in meaningful activism to achieve concrete social change by creating places of strength and unity. These collaborative efforts may empower communities to tackle entrenched disparities and create inclusive and equitable environments. The book's ardent appeal for advocacy served as a strong rallying cry, encouraging readers to utilize their power and stand in solidarity with people oppressed by structural injustices. As readers heed this call to action, they will become catalysts for meaningful change, driving forward a shared vision of a more equitable and compassionate society.

As the pages of this captivating story turn, readers were asked to navigate the complex terrain of controlling anger amid the diverse fabric of culture. With each chapter, the book carefully highlighted the wide range of experiences, struggles, and victories that constitute the human condition. It used moving tales and intelligent analysis to explore the intricacies of negotiating rage in the face of social injustices, institutional disparities, and cultural identity difficulties.

Despite these hurdles, a ray of optimism was found in the resilience inherent in communities and the transformational power of collective action. Through stories of courage, unity, and perseverance, the book vividly depicted individuals and communities rising above hardship and using their fury as a catalyst for genuine change.

As this last chapter concludes, I request a strong call to action to engage in discourse, advocacy, and empowerment efforts. I encourage readers to take an active role in the continuous battle for justice and equality, allowing them to help construct a more inclusive and compassionate society for future generations. Individuals who embrace this invitation are not passive onlookers but active changemakers. They can provide hope and strength that crosses cultural boundaries and creates unity despite variety.

References

Aggarwal, P., Knabel, P., & Fleischer, A. B., Jr. (2021). United States burden of melanoma and non-melanoma skin cancer from 1990 to 2019. *Journal of the American Academy of Dermatology, 85*(2), 388–395. https://doi.org/10.1016/j.jaad.2021.03.109

Alkazemi, M., Ghadikolai, S. O., Oetjens, M., & Boone, E. L. (2021). Attribute agenda setting on Twitter and the Wall Street Journal: The case of Congresswoman Ilhan Omar. *Review of Middle East Studies, 55*(1), 35–55. https://doi.org/10.1017/rms.2021.31

Amodu, O. C., Richter, M. S., & Salami, B. O. (2020). A scoping review of the health of conflict-induced internally displaced women in Africa. *International Journal of Environmental Research and Public Health, 17*(4), 1280–1296. https://doi.org/10.3390/ijerph17041280

Baumgarth, C., Kirkby, A., & Kaibel, C. (2021). When fake becomes real: The innovative case of artificial influencers. In E. Pantano (Ed.), *Creativity and marketing: The fuel for success* (pp. 149–167). Emerald Publishing Limited. https://doi.org10.1108/978-1-80071-330-720211010

Belgrave, F. Z., & Allison, K. W. (2018). *African American psychology: From Africa to America*. Sage Publications.

Blue Bird Jernigan, V., D'Amico, E. J., Duran, B., & Buchwald, D. (2020). Multilevel and community-level interventions with Native Americans: Challenges and opportunities. *Prevention Science, 21*(Suppl 1), 65–73. https://doi.org/10.1007/s11121-018-0916-3

Bowman, E., and Wamsley, L. (2023, November 4). Tens of thousands gather for pro-Palestinian march in D.C. to demand Gaza cease-fire. *Michigan Public*. https://www.michiganpublic.org/2023-11-04/tens-of-thousands-gather-for-pro-palestinian-march-in-d-c-to-demand-gaza-cease-fire

Centers for Disease Control and Prevention. (2022). *Overdose prevention*. https://www.cdc.gov/overdose-prevention/index.html

Centers for Disease Control and Prevention. (2024, April 16). *Mental health: About mental health*. https://www.cdc.gov/mentalhealth/learn/index.htm

Dalfino, D., & Allamneni, S. (2022). *Totalitarianism and individual liberty: A study of contemporary literary texts by Chang, Jung, Julia Alvarez, Svetlana Alexievich, Shirin Ebadi, Divine Dalfino, and Sharada Allamneni* [Online publication]. Vignan's Foundation for Science, Technology & Research. https://www.researchgate.net/profile/Sharada-Allamneni/publication/364225521_Totalitarianism_and_Individual_Liberty_A_Study_of_Contemporary_Literary_Texts_by_Jung_Chang_Julia_Alvarez_Svetlana_Alexievich_and_Shirin_Ebadi/links/633fe5c89cb4fe44f30df240/Totalitarianism-and-Individual-Liberty-A-Study-of-Contemporary-Literary-Texts-by-Jung-Chang-Julia-Alvarez-Svetlana-Alexievich-and-Shirin-Ebadi.pdf

Davis-Undiano, R. C. (2017). *Mestizos come home! Making and claiming Mexican American identity*. University of Oklahoma Press.

Donato, K. M., & Ferris, E. (2020). Refugee integration in Canada, Europe, and the United States: Perspectives from research. *The Annals of the American Academy of Political and Social Science, 690*(1), 7–35. https://doi.org/10.1177/0002716220943169

Durand, J., & Massey, D. S. (2019). Evolution of the Mexico-US migration system: Insights from the Mexican migration project. *The ANNALS of the American Academy of Political and Social Science, 684*(1), 21–42. https://doi.org/10.1177/0002716219857667

The Editors of Encyclopaedia Britannica. (2024). *Shirin Ebadi*. https://www.britannica.com/biography/Shirin-Ebadi

Ellington, T. D., Henley, S. J., Wilson, R. J., Miller, J. W., Wu, M., & Richardson, L. C. (2023). Trends in breast cancer mortality by race/ethnicity, age, and US census region, United States – 1999-2020. *Cancer, 129*(1), 32–38. https://doi.org/10.1002/cncr.34503

Eskin, M., Baydar, N., El-Nayal, M., Asad, N., Noor, I. M., Rezaeian, M., & Khan, M. M. (2020). Associations of religiosity, attitudes towards suicide and religious coping with suicidal ideation and suicide attempts in 11 Muslim countries. *Social Science & Medicine, 265*, 1–11. https://doi.org/10.1016/j.socscimed.2020.113390

Faelens, L., Hoorelbeke, K., Cambier, R., Van Put, J., Van de Putte, E., De Raedt, R., & Koster, E. H. (2021). The relationship between Instagram use and indicators of mental health: A systematic review. *Computers in Human Behavior Reports, 4*, 100–121. https://doi.org/10.1016/j.chbr.2021.100121

References

Golden, A. R., Srisarajivakul, E. N., Hasselle, A. J., Pfund, R. A., & Knox, J. (2023). What was a gap is now a chasm: Remote schooling, the digital divide, and educational inequities resulting from the COVID-19 pandemic. *Current Opinion in Psychology, 52*, Article 101632. https://doi.org/10.1016/j.copsyc.2023.101632

Gonzalez, J. (2022). *Harvest of empire: A history of Latinos in America*. Penguin.

Grubic, A. (2022). Proud: Examining the social media representation of Ibtihaj Muhammad. *Howard Journal of Communications, 33*(4), 396-411. https://doi.org/10.1080/10646175.2022.2027297

Hahm, H. C., Ha, Y., Scott, J. C., Wongchai, V., Chen, J. A., & Liu, C. H. (2021). Perceived COVID-19-related anti-Asian discrimination predicts post-traumatic stress disorder symptoms among Asian and Asian American young adults. *Psychiatry Research, 303*, Article 114084. https://doi.org/10.1016/j.psychres.2021.114084

Hodge, D. R., & Boddie, S. C. (2021). Antisemitism in the United States: An overview and strategies to create a more socially just society. *Social Work, 66*(2), 128–138. https://doi.org/10.1093/sw/swab011

Hwang, W.-C. (2021). Demystifying and addressing internalized racism and oppression among Asian Americans. *American Psychologist, 76*(4), 596–610. https://doi.org/10.1037/amp0000798

Isasi, F., Naylor, M. D., Skorton, D., Grabowski, D. C., Hernández, S., & Rice, V. M. (2021, April 7). Patients, families, and communities COVID-19 impact assessment: Lessons learned and compelling needs [Discussion paper]. *NAM Perspectives*. https://doi.org/10.31478/202111c

Ivey-Stephenson, A., Crosby, A., Jack, S., Haileyesus, T., & Kresnow-Sedacca, M. (2017). Suicide trends among and within urbanization levels by sex, race/ethnicity, age group, and mechanism of death - United States, 2001–2015. *Morbidity and Mortality Weekly Report: Surveillance Summaries, 66*, 1–16. https://doi.org/10.15585/mmwr.ss6618a1

Kehl, M. (2021). Gender representation and journalistic speech: Amal's case. *Cadernos de Gênero e Tecnologia, 14*(44), 129–138. https://doi.org/10.3895/cgt.v14n44.13024

Khan, H., Khan, A., & Bhatti, Z. I. (2021). Politics Of representation, racialization and marginalization in I Am Malala by Christina Lamb and Malala Yousafzai. *Webology, 18*(6), 5995–6005. https://www.webology.org/data-cms/articles/20220713110806amwebology%2018%20(6)%20-%20521.pdf

King, J., John Dennem MA, C. I., & Lockhart, B. (2019). The culture is prevention project: Adapting the Cultural Connectedness Scale for multi-tribal communities. *American Indian and Alaska Native Mental Health Research, 26*(3), 104–135. https://doi.org/10.5820/aian.2603.2019.104

Kirka, D., Hadjicostis, M., & Hussein, F. (2024, January 13). A global day of protests draws thousands in Washington and other cities in pro-Palestinian marches. *AP News.* https://apnews.com/article/protest-gaza-israel-palestinians-london-29d5cd664c81654283344d1874691a4f

Krogstad, J. M., Passel, J. S., Moslimani, M., & Neo-Bustamante, L. (2023, September 22). Key facts about U.S. Latinos for National Hispanic Heritage Month. *Pew Research Center.* https://www.pewresearch.org/short-reads/2023/09/22/key-facts-about-us-latinos-for-national-hispanic-heritage-month/

KSHB News. (2022, September 21). Suicide rates high in middle-aged White men. *Saint Luke's Health System.* https://www.saintlukeskc.org/about/news/kshb-suicide-rates-high-middle-aged-White-men

Kulkami, A. (2024, April 6). Yusra Mardini, Olympian who escaped war-torn Syria by swimming Aegean Sea. *NDTV.* https://www.ndtv.com/people/yusra-mardini-inspiring-journey-olympian-who-escaped-war-torn-syria-by-swimming-aegean-sea-netflix-movie-the-swimmers-5385667

Lagerwey, J. (2018). The Great British Bake Off, joy, and the affective potential of Nadiya Hussain's amateur celebrity. *Celebrity Studies, 9*(4), 442–454. https://doi.org/10.1080/19392397.2018.1508964

Lou, C., Kiew, S. T. J., Chen, T., Lee, T. Y. M., Ong, J. E. C., & Phua, Z. (2023). Authentically fake? How consumers respond to the influence of virtual influencers. *Journal of Advertising, 52*(4), 540–557. https://doi.org/10.1080/00913367.2022.2149641

References

Maddox, T. (2022). "Women were always there…": Caribbean immigrant women, mutual aid societies, and benevolent associations in the early twentieth century. In B. Z. Micheletto (Ed.), *Gender and migration in historical perspective: Institutions, labour and social networks, 16th to 20th centuries* (pp. 485–516). Springer International Publishing. https://doi.org/10.1007/978-3-030-99554-6_15

Magrath, R. (2022). *Athlete activism: Contemporary perspectives*. Routledge.

Maha, B. (2019). Elections, representations, and journalistic schemas: Local news coverage of Ilhan Omar and Rashida Tlaib in the US mid-term elections. *Journal for Communication Studies, 12*(24(2)), 129–146. https://www.essachess.com/index.php/jcs/article/view/467

Mahmud, S., Mohsin, M., Dewan, M. N., & Muyeed, A. (2023). The global prevalence of depression, anxiety, stress, and insomnia among general population during COVID-19 pandemic: A systematic review and meta-analysis. *Trends in Psychology, 31*(1), 143–170. https://doi.org/10.1007/s43076-021-00116-9

March, D. S., Gaertner, L., & Olson, M. A. (2021). Danger or dislike: Distinguishing threat from negative valence as sources of automatic anti-Black bias. *Journal of Personality and Social Psychology, 121*(5), 984–1004. https://doi.org/10.1037/pspa0000288

March, S. (2020). Manufacturing fear: Examining the social component of anti-immigration policies within counter-terrorism discourse. In J. C. Simeon (Ed.), *Terrorism and asylum* (pp. 61–91). Brill Nijhoff.

Mermier, F. (2023). Contemporary Arab media and cultural landscape in Istanbul. In J. F. Khalil, G. Khiabany, T. Guaaybess, & B. Yesil (Eds.), *The handbook of media and culture in the Middle East* (pp. 492–502). Routledge. https://doi.org/10.1002/9781119637134.ch39

Michelini, E. (2021). The representation of Yusra Mardini as a refugee Olympic athlete: A sociological analysis. *Sport und Gesellschaft, 18*(1), 39–64. https://doi.org/10.1515/sug-2021-0003

Moslimani, M., & Noe-Bustamante, L. (2023, August 16). Facts on Latinos in the U.S. *Pew Research Center*. https://www.pewresearch.org/race-and-ethnicity/fact-sheet/latinos-in-the-us-fact-sheet/

The Nobel Prize. (n.d.). *Tawakkol Karman.* https://www.nobelprize.org/events/nobel-prize-summit/2023/panellists/tawakkol-karman-3/#:~:text=During%20the%20Arab%20Spring%2C%20despite,the%202011%20Nobel%20Peace%20Prize

Oates, G., Rutland, S., Juarez, L., Friedman, A., & Schechter, M. S. (2021). The association of area deprivation and state child health with respiratory outcomes of pediatric patients with cystic fibrosis in the United States. *Pediatric Pulmonology, 56*(5), 883–890. https://doi.org/10.3389/fonc.2022.914875

Otto, E. A., Kumar, S. A., & DiLillo, D. (2022). Music's impact on the sexualization of Black bodies: Examining links between hip-hop and sexualization of Black women. *Psi Chi Journal of Psychological Research, 27*(2), 145–153. https://doi.org/10.24839/2325-7342.JN27.2.145

PH, A. R. A., Saputri, W. A., & Nurhakim, P. R. (2023). Socio-religious behavior on consumption pattern during Israel and Palestine conflict in Muslim society. *IAS Journal of Localities, 1*(2), 138–152. https://doi.org/10.62033/iasjol.v1i2.22

Pourrazavi, S., Fathifar, Z., Sharma, M., & Allahverdipour, H. (2023). COVID-19 vaccine hesitancy: A systematic review of cognitive determinants. *Health Promotion Perspectives, 13*(1), 21–35. https://doi.org/10.34172%2Fhpp.2023.03

Rehman, I., & Hanley, T. (2023). Muslim minorities' experiences of Islamophobia in the West: A systematic review. *Culture & Psychology, 29*(1), 139–156. https://doi.org/10.1177/1354067X221103996

Representative of Ilhan Omar (2024, March 1). Focusing on human rights, women's rights and worker's rights were my priorities in Congress in 2023. *Minnesota Post.* https://www.minnpost.com/community-voices/2024/01/ilhan-omar-in-2023-my-focus-was-on-human-rights-in-gaza-green-new-deal-abortion-rights-inflation-reduction-act/

Rosenberg, J. S. (2024, July 23). Harvard antisemitism and anti-Muslim task force reports. *Harvard Magazine.* https://www.harvardmagazine.com/2024/06/harvard-antisemitism-and-anti-muslim-task-force-reports

Ruiz-Esteves, K. N., Teysir, J., Schatoff, D., Elaine, W. Y., & Burnett-Bowie, S. A. M. (2022). Disparities in osteoporosis care among postmenopausal women in the United States. *Maturitas, 156*, 25–29. https://doi.org/10.1016/j.maturitas.2021.10.010

References

Scotland, J., Thomas, A., & Jing, M. (2024). Public emotion and response immediately following the death of George Floyd: A sentiment analysis of social media comments. *Telematics and Informatics Reports, 14*, Article 100143. https://doi.org/10.1016/j.teler.2024.100143

Segev, T. (2024). Israel's forever war: The long history of managing-rather than solving-the conflict. *Foreign Affairs, 103*, 110–118. https://heinonline.org/HOL/LandingPage?handle=hein.journals/fora103&div=50&id=&page=

Seigel, J. (2019, February 20). Rural hospital closures rise to ninety-eight. *National Rural Health Association.* https://www.ruralhealth.us/blogs/2019/02/rural-hospital-closures-rise-to-ninety-eight

Siegel, R. L., Wagle, N. S., Cercek, A., Smith, R. A., & Jemal, A. (2023). Colorectal cancer statistics, 2023. *CA: A Cancer Journal for Clinicians, 73*(3), 233–254. https://doi.org/10.3322/caac.21772

Statista. (n.d.). *Hispanic population groups in the United States in 2022, by country of origin.* https://www.statista.com/statistics/234852/us-hispanic-population/#:~:text=As%20of%202022%2C%20around%2037.41,the%20U.S.%20in%20that%20year

Stern Milch, C. (2023, May 11). Read Amal Clooney's powerful speech for the Cartier Women's Initiative Awards: 'Justice must be waged'. *Elle.* https://www.elle.com/culture/celebrities/a43856181/amal-clooney-cartier-womens-initiative-speech-transcript/

Tineo, P., Bonumwezi, J. L., & Lowe, S. R. (2021). Discrimination and posttraumatic growth among Muslim American youth: Mediation via posttraumatic stress disorder symptoms. *Journal of Trauma & Dissociation, 22*(2), 188–201. https://doi.org/10.1080/15299732.2020.1869086

Underferth, D. (2019, February). Your breast cancer risk: How it's affected by race. *The University of Texas: MD Anderson Cancer Center.* https://www.mdanderson.org/publications/focused-on-health/your-breast-cancer-risk--how-it-s-affected-by-race-.h11-1592991.html#:~:text=About%201%20in%208%20women,same%20rate%20at%20around%2012%25

U.S. Holocaust Memorial Museum. (n.d.-a). *Animated map: World War II and the Holocaust.* https://encyclopedia.ushmm.org/content/en/animated-map/world-war-ii-and-the-holocaust

U.S. Holocaust Memorial Museum. (n.d.-b). *World War II and the Holocaust (1939–1945)*. https://www.ushmm.org/learn/holocaust/world-war-ii-and-the-holocaust-1939-1945

Von Sikorski, C., Schmuck, D., Matthes, J., & Binder, A. (2020). "Muslims are not terrorists": Islamic state coverage, journalistic differentiation between terrorism and Islam, fear reactions, and attitudes toward Muslims. In S. S. Fahmy (Ed.), *Media, terrorism and society: Perspectives and trends in the Digital Age* (pp. 91–114). Routledge. https://doi.org/10.4324/9780429433016-6

Wang, S. C., Raja, A. H., & Azhar, S. (2020). "A lot of us have a very difficult time reconciling what being Muslim is": A phenomenological study on the meaning of being Muslim American. *Cultural Diversity and Ethnic Minority Psychology, 26*(3), 338–346. https://doi.org/10.1037/cdp0000297

Waters, M. C. (2022). Ethnic and racial identities of second-generation Black immigrants in New York City. In M. M. Suárez-Orozco, C. Suárez-Orozco, & D. Qin-Hilliard (Eds.), *The new immigrants and American schools* (pp. 227–252). Routledge.

White, A. M. (2020). Gender differences in the epidemiology of alcohol use and related harms in the United States. *Alcohol Research: Current Reviews, 40*(2), 1–10. https://doi.org/10.35946/arcr.v40.2.01

Yin, S. (2018, August 1). Elderly White men afflicted by high suicide rates. *Population Reference Bureau.* https://www.prb.org/resources/elderly-White-men-afflicted-by-high-suicide-rates/

www.ingramcontent.com/pod-product-compliance
Lightning Source LLC
Chambersburg PA
CBHW050636160426
43194CB00010B/1691